Roadmap to Success –

5 Steps to Putting Action into your Affirmative Action Program

By

Thomas H. Nail

Cornelia Gamlem, SPHR

Cover designed by: Erik Gamlem
Big Heavy Design
www.bigheavydesign.com

Roadmap to Success –

5 Steps to Putting Action into your Affirmative Action Program

Thomas H. Nail
President

THOMAS HOUSTON associates, inc.
620 Herndon Parkway, Suite 200
Herndon, VA 20170
(703) 481-9839
e-mail: thnail@thomashouston.com
web-site: www.thomashouston.com

Cornelia Gamlem, SPHR
President

GEMS Group ltd
PO Box 148
Herndon, VA 20172
(703) 709-9114
e-mail: cornelia@gemsgroup-hr.com
website: www.gemsgroup-hr.com

Roadmap to Success – 5 Steps to Putting Action into your Affirmative Action Program (Roadmap) is published only as an informational guide. The reader should keep in mind that although this *Roadmap* is designed to provide accurate and current information on employment law compliance issues as of the date of publication, the information contained herein is general in nature and is not intended to be relied upon as legal advice. The resolution of each circumstance encountered by readers of this *Roadmap* would ultimately be determined on a case by case basis, depending upon the particular facts presented, and legal counsel should also be consulted as appropriate. THOMAS HOUSTON associates, inc. and GEMS Group ltd welcomes the opportunity to discuss in greater detail the information set forth in this book and how it might apply to the specific needs of your company.

DEDICATION

This book is dedicated to our spouses, Candyce Nail and Carl Gamlem, and our sons, Alex and Christopher Nail and Erik Gamlem who share our "road trips" and "life journeys".

Table of Contents

INTRODUCTION TO THE ROADMAP

The Department of Labor's Office of Federal Contract Compliance Program (OFCCP) has increased its emphasis on affirmative action compliance. Compliance will be measured by the extent to which a company identifies problem areas within employment processes and how the identified problem areas are addressed within the affirmative action program to ensure that all individuals have equal access to all employment opportunities.

The first step in developing an affirmative action program should be a review of the results of the affirmative action plan. Action-oriented programs should be crafted for the coming affirmative action program year addressing the specific problem areas identified in the plan.

This roadmap provides a model for developing an affirmative action program by providing a clearer understanding of the responsibilities and requirement of affirmative action compliance as well as practical guidance toward the execution of a successful affirmative action program. It explains the distinction between an affirmative action plan and the broader affirmative action program. It also explains the distinction between discrimination and affirmative action. Finally, it is a guide through the required elements of affirmative action compliance that includes checklists for self-evaluation of program compliance.

The information provided in this roadmap is general in nature and it is not intended to be relied upon as legal advice. In addition, the information contained herein is presented as guidance and is not a guarantee of a successful outcome in the event of an OFCCP compliance evaluation. Each compliance evaluation involves a unique set of variables; therefore the outcome of each compliance evaluation is unique. Expert advice from consultants and legal counsel should be obtained as appropriate.

STEP 1 – REVIEWING THE BASICS

Companies that transact a minimum of $50,000 per year in business with the federal government and who employ at least 50 full-time or part-time employees are prohibited from engaging in discriminatory employment practices, required to prepare a written affirmative action plan each year, and implement the affirmative action program in accordance with specific governing regulations

During compliance evaluations, the Department of Labor's Office of Federal Contract Compliance Program (OFCCP) audits the written affirmative action plan for technical compliance and more importantly, audits the entire affirmative action program to determine if the compliance standards contained in the regulations are being met.

Executive Order 11246 prohibits discrimination against individuals on the basis of race, color, religion, sex, or national origin. Under Executive Order 11246, a contractor is required to implement affirmative action plans in order to increase female and minority participation in the workplace. The Rehabilitation Act of 1973 prohibits discrimination against individuals on the basis of mental or physical disability, and requires that the contractor take affirmative action to employ and promote qualified disabled individuals. Likewise, the Vietnam Era Veterans' Readjustment Assistance Act of 1974 prohibits discrimination against qualified disabled veterans, Vietnam era veterans, and other categories of protected veterans, and requires that a contractor take affirmative action to employ such veterans and advance them in their employment.

The implementing rules and regulations for these laws are written by the OFCCP. These regulations are found in 41 CFR, Chapter 60. The regulations governing Executive Order 11246 are discussed in Step 1 through Step 4 of this roadmap. The requirements for individuals with disabilities and certain covered veterans are discussed in Step 5.

DISCRIMINATION VERSUS AFFIRMATIVE ACTION

Discrimination

Companies must refrain from making any employment or personnel decision on the basis of race, color, religion, sex, national origin, age, disability, or veteran status. Equal Employment Opportunity (EEO) refers to a company's efforts to ensure nondiscrimination. Discrimination is:

- providing intentional preferential treatment to one individual or group of individuals over others because of their membership in a certain group (adverse treatment or intentional discrimination); or
- engaging in employment practices which result in one group being favored over another group (adverse impact discrimination).

Affirmative Action

Companies are required to engage in specific activities to ensure that groups protected by civil rights law (protected groups or classes) have the opportunity to be hired, advanced in employment, and compensated equally.

Affirmative Action is:
- providing equal employment opportunities for all individuals
- giving full consideration to members of protected classes in all areas of employment
- monitoring the workforce to identify areas where protected classes are not fully represented or utilized
- going beyond EEO efforts to take pro-active steps to attract and retain protected groups

Affirmative Action is not:
- providing preferences to protected groups
- interpreting "full consideration" as a "requirement" to advance in employment less qualified members of protected groups
- the use of quotas

THE AFFIRMATIVE ACTION PLAN VERSUS THE AFFIRMATIVE ACTION PROGRAM

Affirmative Action Plan

An affirmative action plan is a management tool that documents a company's on-going efforts including the results of certain quantitative analyses. This plan or "tool" is designed to assist in affirmative action efforts and it should be used in a diagnostic manner to enhance a company's commitment to EEO/ Affirmative Action.

The plan must be updated annually; writing the plan is an event.

Affirmative Action Program

An affirmative action program is a company's effort to ensure equal employment opportunity within its employment and human resources policies, practices and processes. It institutionalizes a company's commitment to affirmative action. The OFCCP expects that it is part of the way that a company regularly conducts its business.

The program is the way in which a company conducts business; it is a process rather than an event.

4

HOW TO USE THIS ROADMAP

This roadmap was designed to assist a company in effectively developing its affirmative action program. It provides practical guidance on those activities that support a company's commitment to equal employment opportunity. Certain activities are required under the regulations. Others are more focused to meet an individual company's or individual plan's needs.

This roadmap will not teach how to write the affirmative action plan, nor does it provide a detailed explanation of how to conduct the statistical elements described in 41 CFR§ 60-2.11 through 2.16 as discussed in Step 2.

The roadmap provides:

- An overview of the regulations, along with explanations of what is expected by the OFCCP to develop the company's program.
- Key observations to supplement these explanations of the regulations. They are intended to help in auditing the company's HR processes and practices.
- Detailed checklists that contain specific actions generally acknowledged as affirmative action efforts that will assist in removing barriers to equal employment opportunity. The checklists should be used to streamline and focus the coordination and implementation of affirmative action efforts.

Note: Many of the checklists that appear in this roadmap, particularly those within Step 3, represent a wide array of items that a company can engage in to support EEO and affirmative action. In reviewing these checklists, keep in mind that they are provided as guidance, and do not necessarily represent a mandate to incorporate all the items into the company's affirmative action program. Things such as the size of the company, the nature of the industry, and the market factors at any given time must be considered. Don't factor judgment out of the process of developing the company's affirmative action program.

• Appendices that provide more detailed instructions on certain topical areas as well as a glossary of terms for reference.

STEP 2 – UNDERSTANDING THE REGULATIONS

AFFIRMATIVE ACTION PROGRAMS FOR MINORITIES & FEMALES (41 CFR§60-2)

The regulations governing Affirmative Action provide two standards for determining compliance: **Nondiscrimination Compliance** and **Affirmative Action Compliance**.

Nondiscrimination Compliance

Nondiscrimination compliance is determined by the analysis of statistical data and other non-statistical information that would indicate fair and nondiscriminatory treatment. The statistical data is generally covered in the affirmative action plan by addressing the obligations under the following requirements:

41 CFR§60-2.1 ORGANIZATIONAL PROFILE

- Depicts staffing patterns to help identify under-representation or concentration and barriers to equal employment
- Can be either an organizational display or workforce analysis

    Organizational Display

    - Detailed graphical or tabular chart, text, spreadsheet or similar presentation of contractor's organizational structure
    - Identifies each organizational unit in establishment and shows relationship of each to others
    - Contains aggregated race/ethnicity/gender data for incumbents

Workforce Analysis

- Must contain a listing of each job title in the organizational unit ranked from lowest paid to highest paid. For each job title, the analysis must include, the wage rate or salary range and the number of incumbents by race, ethnicity, and gender

41 CFR§60-2.12   JOB GROUP ANALYSIS

- Combines jobs "at the establishment" with similar content, wage rates, and opportunities
- Must include a list of the job titles that comprise each job group
- Must be annotated and cross-referenced for jobs located at another establishment
- Smaller employers may use EEO-1 categories (contractors with total workforce less than 150 employees)

41 CFR§60-2.13   PLACEMENT OF INCUMBENTS IN JOB GROUP

- Must separately state percentage of minorities and percentage of females employed in each job group as defined in the job group analysis prepared in accordance with 41 CFR§60-2.12.

41 CFR§60-2.14   DETERMINING AVAILABILITY

- Defines availability as an estimate of the number of qualified minorities or females available for employment
- Must be expressed as a percentage of those minorities or females qualified to perform the jobs within a job group.
- Requires the use of at least two factors to determine availability
  - External availability (recruiting areas)- local and expanded
  - Internal availability - employees promotable, transferable, and trainable within the organization

8

41 CFR§60-2.15 COMPARING INCUMBENCY TO AVAILABILITY

- Requires placement goals be set for all job groups where the percentage of minorities or females employed in each job group (job group analysis) is less than would reasonably be expected given availability (availability analysis)

41 CFR§60-2.16 PLACEMENT GOALS

- Defined as objectives or targets reasonably attainable by applying every good faith effort
  - Percentage annual placement goal must be at least equal to availability
  - Requires single goal for all minorities. OFCCP may require goals for minority subgroups if substantial disparity exists

In addition to performing these analyses, there are additional requirements under 41 CFR§60-2.17 for affirmative action compliance. Those required elements of affirmative action programs are discussed next.

Affirmative Action Compliance

Affirmative action compliance is measured by the *nature and extent* of activities under 41 CFR§60-2.17, "Additional required elements of affirmative action programs." These additional requirements are explained below. Tools and guidance for assuring affirmative action compliance are the basics of this roadmap.

41 CFR §60-2.17(a) DESIGNATION OF RESPONSIBILITY

This section requires that a specific individual within the company be assigned the role of EEO Official, Officer, or Coordinator. This individual will be responsible and accountable for the implementation of the affirmative action program and ensuring that the policies and practices supporting the program are properly executed. This individual must have the authority, resources, support, and access to top management to ensure the effective implementation of the affirmative action program. This individual will serve as a liaison between the company and enforcement agencies.

The EEO Official/Officer/Coordinator responsibilities encompass all areas discussed in the checklist in this section.

41 CFR§60-2.17(b)   IDENTIFICATION OF PROBLEM AREAS

In-depth analyses of the total employment process are required to determine whether and where impediments to equal employment opportunity exist. At minimum, a company must complete two categories of analyses:

quantitative analysis:
- Workforce by organizational unit and job group
- Personnel activity (applicant flow, hires, terminations, promotions, and other personnel actions)
- Compensation systems

qualitative analysis:
- Selection recruitment, referral and other personnel procedures

A more detailed and expanded discussions of these analyses are contained in Steps 3 and 4. These discussions are supported by key observations to assist in evaluating each completed analysis and checklists to assist in **tailoring** action-oriented programs to **specific** problem areas identified.

41 CFR§60-2.17(c) ACTION-ORIENTED PROGRAMS

The OFCCP requires that companies develop and execute action-oriented programs designed to correct any potential problem areas identified pursuant to 41 CFR§60-2.17(b) and to attain established goals and objectives. The OFCCP further requires that action-oriented programs "consist of more than following the same procedures that have previously produced inadequate results."

The implementation of these action-oriented programs will result in the practice of good faith efforts. Good faith efforts are defined by the OFCCP as "demonstrated efforts to remove identified barriers, expand employment opportunities, and produce measurable results." Good faith efforts are crucial to the success of an Affirmative Action Program. The documented practice of good faith efforts will positively impact the final results of an OFCCP Compliance Evaluation. Documentation must be maintained on all action-oriented programs that include the practice of good faith efforts. In the event of an OFCCP Compliance Evaluation, supporting documentation of stated activities will be required. With the OFCCP's emphasis on implementing action-oriented programs that produce measurable results, it is important that program development is tailored to the problem areas identified in each affirmative action plan.

A checklist of "Broad Good Faith Efforts" and action-oriented programs is included in this section. The items contained in the checklists are **general approaches** that companies may use in developing their action-oriented programs. In the event of a compliance evaluation, the OFCCP will require specific details and supporting documentation of action-oriented programs and good faith efforts.

11

CHECKLIST: 41 CFR§60-2.17(a) Designation of Responsibility – EEO Official/Officer/Coordinator Responsibilities

❏ Develop and implement the Affirmative Action Program and review the results with management.

❏ Develop, implement, and maintain the audit and reporting systems to measure the program's effectiveness.

❏ Advise managers in the modification and development of EEO policies and programs for all employees within existing laws, regulations, and guidelines.

❏ Serve as a liaison between minority and female organizations and community action groups that are concerned with employment opportunities for minorities, females, US Veterans, and persons with disabilities.

❏ Assist management in identifying problem areas and establishing local Affirmative Action Program goals and objectives.

❏ Supervise recruitment efforts to ensure that the pre-employment process is free of discriminatory procedures.

❏ Perform periodic audits of selection and training practices to remove impediments to attaining Affirmative Action Program goals and objectives.

❏ Perform periodic audits to ensure that posters are properly displayed, thereby ensuring that minority and female employees are informed of their rights.

❏ Ensure that minority and female employees are afforded the opportunity and are encouraged to participate in all company-sponsored educational, training, recreational, and social activities.

❏ Hold periodic discussions with managers, supervisors, and employees to ensure that EEO and affirmative action policies are being followed.

❏ Review the qualifications of all employees to ensure that minorities and females are provided full opportunities for transfers and promotions.

❏ Ensure that employees are provided with career counseling.

❏ Make management aware that their work performance evaluation is based partially on their EEO efforts and is part of their annual performance review.

❏ Guide managers in taking proper action to prevent employees from being harassed by other employees or managers.

❏ Work closely with minority and female recruiting sources, state employment offices, rehabilitation and service centers, advising these recruiting sources of the company's EEO policy.

❏ Ensure that all new employees are briefed on the EEO policy at the time of orientation and are familiar with the affirmative action program and its objectives.

❏ Analyze applicant flow periodically with respect to race and gender to ensure there is adequate representation of minorities and females in the candidate pool.

❏ Establish recruiting and advertising strategies in minority and female-oriented publications.

❏ Ensure that all employment decisions are consistent with EEO policy.

❏ Review all job descriptions to ensure that they are free of discrimination provisions and reflect the actual requirements of the work to be performed.

❑ Ensure that internal promotion and transfer of all employees is consistent with the affirmative action goals and objectives.

❑ Periodically review the use of benefits, social and recreational programs, and the facility in general to ensure equal opportunity.

❑ Review compensation systems to ensure equitable pay practices consistent with policies and procedures.

CHECKLIST: 41 CFR§60-2.17(c) Action-Oriented Programs – Broad Good Faith Efforts

An evaluation of the demonstrated good faith efforts of action-oriented programs should be conducted on an annual basis to determine if they have been effective. The majority of the good faith efforts listed below are those that the OFCCP would like to see in affirmative action programs and plans. Consideration should be given to the practices listed below that are not currently part of an affirmative action program that may be incorporated as part of the coming program year. Some of the items listed below may not be practical for all companies.

❑ Enroll in an OFCCP Liaison Group.

❑ Develop policy statements, affirmative action programs and internal and external communication techniques.

❑ Review the requirements contained in 41 CFR§60-20 - Sex Discrimination Guidelines to evaluate the company's policies and practices against these regulations.

❑ Review the requirements contained in 41 CFR§60-50 – Guidelines on Discrimination Because of Region or National Origin to evaluate the company's policies and practices against these regulations.

❑ Monitor all recruitment activity and sources to ensure that the applicant pool is representative of the availability of minorities and females and free from discriminatory practices.

❑ Send open positions notifications to all recruitment sources including community agencies that support minorities and females.

❑ Conduct periodic audits to ensure posters and policies are current and properly displayed.

❑ Conduct periodic audits to ensure that all employment-related forms meet federal and state EEO requirements.

❏ Ensure that seniority practices do not have a discriminatory effect.

❏ Assign EEO/affirmative action responsibilities to line management and include the evaluation of equal employment opportunity efforts and results in performance evaluations.

❏ Ensure that the company has developed and implemented a harassment policy and that such a policy is enforced.

❏ Develop and implement an Educational Assistance Program and communicate the availability to all employees (i.e. employee handbook, newsletters, payroll stuffers, intranet, Company web site, etc.)

❏ Monitor the educational assistance program to ensure that minorities and females have equal access and opportunity to use the program.

❏ Review Human Resources practices to ensure that they are nondiscriminatory and administered fairly and consistently.

❏ Inform all individuals in management positions of their responsibilities regarding equal employment opportunity and related policies and practices during management meetings.

❏ Conduct briefings with all levels for management to discuss the progress of the affirmative action program, including the status of specific goals.

❏ Develop and implement a Diversity Program.

❏ Develop and implement an Employee Assistance Program and communicate the availability to all employees (i.e. employee handbook, newsletters, payroll stuffers, intranet, Company web site, etc.)

❏ Publish articles covering EEO programs, as well as promotions, accomplishments etc., of minority and female employees in Company publications (i.e. newsletters, intranet, Company web site, etc.)

❏ Include pictures of both minority and non-minority males and females when employees are featured in internal Company publications (i.e. newsletters, employee handbook, training manuals, intranet, Company web site, etc.)

❏ Actively encourage all employees to participate in Company sponsored social and recreational activities (i.e. Company picnics, sports leagues, etc.)

❏ Develop and utilize workforce flexibility programs in order to attract and retain employees. (i.e. childcare, transportation, flex time, job rotation, buddy system and similar programs)

❏ Initiate remedial, job training and work-study programs.

❏ Consistently sponsor membership of employees involved in professional organizations ensuring that minorities and females have equal opportunity to participate in this benefit.

❏ Conduct employee satisfaction surveys on a periodic basis.

❏ Inform minority and female organizations, community agencies, and community leaders of the Company's affirmative action policy in writing.

❏ Develop and adhere to a schedule for the periodic review and update of position descriptions to ensure they are consistent with business necessity and include only valid job-related requirements.

❏ Utilize consistent position requirements for all employment selection processes.

❏ Ensure that employment testing (if used) is consistent, validated and nondiscriminatory. (i.e. EEO, ADA)

❏ Actively support local and national community action programs and community service programs designed to improve the employment opportunities for minorities and females. (i.e. financial and/or employee participation)

❏ Encourage the participation of employees, especially minorities and females, in youth motivation programs. (i.e. Career Days, Jr. Achievement, Employee Shadowing Programs, Mentoring Programs, Work Study Programs)

❏ Assist secondary schools and colleges in the design of programs to enable minority and female graduates to compete in the open employment market. (i.e. interview skills, resume skills)

❏ Develop and utilize summer employment programs that promote the employment of minority and female youths.

❏ Include minority and non-minority males and females when employees are featured in external Company publications. (i.e. consumer, product or employment advertising)

❏ Publicize the achievements of minority and female employees in appropriate local minority and female news media. (Contact Chamber of Commerce for listing of local media.)

CHECKLIST: 41 CFR§60-1 Obligations of Contractors and Subcontractors – Equal Opportunity

The Government wants to ensure that all of its contractors promote and ensure equal opportunity for all persons, without regard to protected class. Doing business with the government makes the government the company's customer, and the government, as a customer, imposes certain "customer service" obligations upon its contractors. These obligations focus on issues such as policy development and publicity, maintaining records and filing required reports, and assuring that all entities with which the company does business understand and practice equal employment opportunity requirements. These obligations are outlined in the checklist below. In the event of an OFCCP Compliance Evaluation, documentation is necessary as proof of meeting the obligations listed.

❑ Include the required equal employment opportunity clause on all Government contracts or subcontracts

❑ Include the EEO/AA tag line in all employment advertising. (EOE/AA/MFDV)

❑ Post all pertinent policies on Company bulletin boards. (i.e. EEO, Affirmative Action, Harassment, Leave of Absence)

❑ Notify union(s) of the existence of the Affirmative Action Plan and union obligations under the plan. (i.e. nondiscrimination clauses in all union agreements, annual union letter)

❑ Include the required equal employment opportunity clause on all subcontracts and purchase orders.

❑ File the EEO-1 report annually.

❑ File the VETS-100 report annually.

❑ Conduct periodic audits of all Company facilities to ensure that they are desegregated as well as comparable for both genders. (i.e. rest room, locker rooms)

❏ Keep all personnel or employment records on file for a period of not less than two years.

❏ Maintain a current AAP and documentation and retain the immediately preceding AAP.

❏ Identify and maintain the gender, race, and ethnicity of each employee and applicant. (Refer to the EEO-1 instruction booklet for current race/ ethnic categories.).

❏ Request race and gender self ID information from all applicants in order to monitor hiring selection decisions. (i.e. application/web site tear sheet, visual identification)

❏ Include the EEO policy statement in the Affirmative Action Plan.

❏ Post the EEO policy statement on Company bulletin boards

❏ Develop and implement an audit and reporting system that will measure the success of the Affirmative Action Program.

❏ Take any necessary action to address identified deficiencies in the Affirmative Action Program (i.e. implement action-oriented programs)

❏ Train all personnel involved in selection, disciplinary and related processes to eliminate the potential for bias and ensure that the Affirmative Action Program is properly implemented (i.e. interview, hire, promotion, discipline, termination, etc.

❏ Utilize local chapters of organizations of and for minorities and females to attract individuals who have the requisite skills and can be recruited through affirmative action measures.

❏ Make available minorities and females for participation in career days, youth motivation programs, and related activities in their communities.

INTERNAL DISSEMINATION OF POLICY:

(The OFCCP does not "contemplate that contractors will necessarily undertake all the activities listed.")

❏	Include all pertinent policies in the Employee Handbook. (i.e. EEO, Affirmative Action, Harassment, Leave of Absence)

❏	Include all pertinent policies in the Company Policy Manual. (i.e. EEO, Affirmative Action, Harassment, Leave of Absence)

❏	Periodically inform all employees and prospective employees of the Company's commitment to EEO/affirmative action (i.e. posting the EEO policy, payroll stuffers, operational training programs, etc.)

❏	Schedule meetings with all employees to discuss the Company's policies and commitment and explain individual employee responsibilities. (i.e. EEO, Affirmative Action, Harassment, Leave of Absence)

❏	Publicize pertinent policies in Company publications (i.e. newsletter, intranet, Company web site, annual report, etc.)

❏	Notify employees of the name and phone number of the EEO Official/ Officer/Coordinator.

❏	Notify executive, management, and supervisory personnel of the intent of affirmative action and the individual responsibility for effective implementation, making clear the Company's attitude (i.e. scheduled meetings, periodic correspondence directed to appropriate individuals, etc. Document all meetings with minutes that include a list of attendees.)

❏	Discuss the Company's policies and commitments in new hire orientation programs. (i.e. EEO, Affirmative Action, Harassment, Leave of Absence)

❏ Discuss the Company's policies and commitments in management training programs. (i.e. EEO, Affirmative Action, Harassment, Leave of Absence)

❏ Meet with union officials and/or employee representatives to inform them of the Company's policy, and request their cooperation.

❏ Include articles on the accomplishments of minority and female employees in Company publications.

❏ Include minority and female employees when employees are featured in internal Company publications (i.e. newsletters, employee handbook, training manuals, intranet, web site, etc.)

EXTERNAL DISSEMINATION OF POLICY, OUTREACH AND POSITIVE RECRUITMENT:

(The OFCCP does not "contemplate that contractors will necessarily undertake all the activities listed.")

❏ Enlist assistance and support of specialized recruiting sources representing minorities and females to provide meaningful employment opportunities to qualified individuals.

❏ Conduct formal briefing sessions with representatives from specialized recruiting sources including: plant tours, clear and concise explanations of current and future job openings, position descriptions, worker specifications, and explanations of the Company's selection process. Make formal arrangements for referral of applicants, follow up with sources, and feedback on disposition of applicants.

❏ Inform all recruiting sources, including placement firms and schools and colleges, verbally and in writing, of the Company's commitment to EEO and affirmative action.

❏ Establish meaningful contacts with appropriate social service agencies and organizations of and for minorities and females for technical assistance and referral of potential employees.

❏ Inform appropriate social service agencies and organizations representing the interests of minorities and females of the Company's EEO and affirmative action policy in writing.

❏ Include minorities and females when employees are featured in external Company publications. (i.e. consumer, promotional, or employment advertising)

❏ Notify all subcontractors, vendors, and suppliers, in writing, of Company's affirmative action commitment, requesting appropriate action on their part.

STEP 3 - EVALUATING THE QUANTITATIVE ANALYSES

41 CFR§60-2.17(b)(1) WORKFORCE BY ORGANIZATIONAL UNIT

Job Area Acceptance Range (JAAR) Analysis

The workforce must be evaluated by organization unit to determine whether there are problems of minority or female distribution; that is, whether minorities and females are spread evenly throughout the company's workforce or whether they are concentrated or underrepresented in certain areas of the company or in certain types of jobs.

The JAAR (Job Area Acceptance Range) Analysis is **one** method of evaluating the workforce by organizational units (e.g. departments). The JAAR Analysis compares the total company workforce contained in the Affirmative Action Plan to individual segments of that workforce. An individual segment may be a department or any organizational unit selected to be analyzed. The idea is that the distribution of females and minorities in the individual segment should be similar to that of the distribution of females and minorities in the total workforce. A JAAR Analysis or some other method of analyzing workforce distribution should be performed at least annually as part of the affirmative action plan.

Please refer to *Appendix C* for more information on how to calculate the JAAR.

41 CFR§60-2.17(b)(1) WORKFORCE BY JOB GROUP

Utilization Analysis

The Utilization Analysis evaluates a workforce by job group (e.g. Officials and Managers, Professionals, Clerical). The analysis compares the percentage of incumbent minorities and females in each job group with the protected class availability for those job groups. Where the percentage of minorities or females employed in a particular job group is less than would reasonably be expected given their availability percentage in that particular job group, placement rate goals must be established. (Refer to Step 2, Nondiscrimination Compliance) Underutilization is the term that historically has identified those job groups where the representation of minorities and females is less than reasonably expected (less than 80% or greater than -2.0 standard deviations). In addition to setting placement rate goals, action-oriented programs must be implemented to address areas of underutilization. The Utilization Analysis must be performed at least annually as part of the affirmative action plan.

Where underutilization exists, the OFCCP will expect that the pool of qualified minority and female applicants be increased through positive outreach (See *Appendix B*)

They will also expect an increase in the number of qualified minority and females within feeder jobs. Feeder jobs lead to positions in higher-level job groups.

41 CFR§60-2.17(b)(2) PERSONNEL ACTIVITY

Impact Ratio Analysis (IRA)

The Impact Ratio Analysis (IRA) is a method of analyzing personnel activity by job groups and must be performed at least annually as part of the affirmative action plan. When writing the Affirmative Action Plan, personnel activity for the 12-month period <u>preceding</u> the start the new plan year must be analyzed. In the event of a compliance evaluation by the OFCCP, additional analysis of personnel activity that occurred since the start of the affirmative action plan year may be required if the compliance evaluation takes place at least six months into the <u>current</u> plan year. The IRA may also be conducted quarterly or semi-annually for any or all job groups. The IRA:

- determines the rate of selection for minorities and the rate of selection for non-minorities
- compares the minority selection rate to the non-minority selection rate
- determines the rate of selection for females and the rate of selection for males
- compares the female selection rate to the male selection rate

The results of the comparison may be an indicator of discriminatory practices. Statistically significant adverse impact (i.e. greater than -2.0 standard deviations) is considered an indicator of potential discrimination. The OFCCP is interested in any incident of selection disparities, not just statistically significant disparities.

Each area of indicated adverse impact must be researched to determine why it exists for each personnel activity and to ensure that no discriminatory decisions were made.

The IRA is <u>typically</u> conducted to analyze the personnel activity listed below. Depending on the size and nature of the workforce and the types of activity experienced, the scope of this analysis may be expanded to include employment offers, declinations, or training opportunities.

- New Hires versus Applicant Flow
- Promotions versus Incumbent Workforce
- Terminations and/or Layoffs versus Incumbent Workforce

The OFCCP usually focuses on those terminations that were involuntary since they represent employment decisions made by the company. Depending on the amount of activity, it may be advisable to analyze layoff activity separate from other involuntary terminations.

Analyzing voluntary terminations, which are decisions made by the employees and generally out of the company's control, is not required. This analysis, however, may indicate potential issues related to employee retention and turnover. Documentation of voluntary resignations should be maintained in the employee's personnel file.

Please refer to *Appendix D* for more information on how to calculate the IRA.

41 CFR§60-2.17(b)(3) COMPENSATION SYSTEMS

Compensation analysis, or pay equity, has become an extremely important issue in recent OFCCP compliance evaluations. A company must be prepared to address compensation issues in detail. Companies are prohibited from discriminating in their compensation practices and an analysis of compensation systems is required under 41 CFR§60-2.17(b)(3).

A company must analyze pay practices and research instances where minorities and/or females are paid less than non-minorities and/or males who are performing the same or substantially the same jobs. More than likely, there will be situations where some degree of disparity exists. This is not, however, an indication that discrimination necessarily exists. There may be several bona fide, job-related reasons for a difference in pay between individuals.

For example:

- Education
- Total work experience
- Seniority
- Time in job
- Performance
- Specialized job knowledge
- Specialized training
- Reassignment without pay reduction, red circling
- Company acquisitions, mergers, or restructuring
- Geographic location

When pay disparities are identified, it is important to examine each situation and determine if the disparity is due to bona fide, job-related reasons. If bona fide, job-related reasons cannot be identified and supported, then a presumption of discrimination will exist. The examples listed above are some of the legitimate, nondiscriminatory reasons for pay differences. This list is not intended to be all-inclusive and there may be additional explanations.

A meaningful analysis of the pay practices and identification of any apparent disparity may be completed by following the Cohort Analysis procedure outlined in *Appendix E*. In analyzing a large workforce, it may be helpful to use an electronic spreadsheet application.

For job titles with 30 or more incumbents and five (5) or more incumbents of a protected group, statistical methodologies may be used to determine whether differences in pay are statistically significant. Two such methodologies are standard deviation and rank sum analysis. A discussion of how to calculate standard deviation and rank sum analysis is outside the scope of this roadmap.

A compensation system may be justified through the use of job descriptions and job evaluation methodologies. These methods can explain differences in jobs and provide documentation to support compensation decisions.

KEY OBSERVATIONS – JAAR Analysis

A high concentration of protected classes in middle management jobs and/or an under-representation in top management jobs as represented by functional departments may indicate a "glass ceiling".

A marked difference in female representation in the white and blue-collar workforce totals may be an indicator that "gender" placements are being made based on traditional custom or practice (i.e. males placed as truck drivers, females placed as secretaries).

An under-representation or concentration of protected classes within a segment should prompt an examination of the placement practices within the identified segment ensuring that no discriminatory situations exist (i.e. managerial bias, artificial steering of protected classes into job areas that are typically lower paid or lower level positions).

An imbalance of individual minority representation within a segment should prompt an examination of the placement practices within the identified segment ensuring that no managerial bias exists.

When an under-representation of a protected class is indicated in a segment, refer to the availability figures and goal objectives for jobs in that department. Low availability percentages may be the direct contributing factor to under-representation.

KEY OBSERVATIONS – Utilization Analysis

A high concentration of protected classes in middle management jobs and an under-representation in top management jobs may indicate a "glass ceiling."

A high-utilization of females in the clerical job groups may indicate that "gender" placements are being made based on traditional custom or practice.

Job groups with fractional underutilization (shortfall of less than one person) should be noted as watchpoints.

Job groups where the protected class incumbency is 0% should be noted as watchpoints.

Job groups where the utilization of protected groups exceeds availability (parity) may provide promotional opportunities to job groups where underutilization exists.

KEY OBSERVATIONS – Impact Ratio Analysis

Determine if the number of protected class applicants truly reflects availability

Observe the job groups in which adverse impact exists.

Determine whether any discernable patterns to the adverse impact are evident

Determine whether the adverse impact exists for a specific covered group

The IRA serves to identify possible problem areas where the selection rate for minorities and for females is less than 80% of the selection rate for non-minorities or males for positive employment actions (hiring, promotions, and training)

The IRA also serves to identify possible problem areas where the selection rate for minorities and/or females is greater than 120% of the selection rate for non-minorities or males for negative employment actions (terminations and layoffs)

Situations where apparent adverse impact exists must be investigated to identify potential problem areas

Written justification for each selection decision which caused apparent adverse impact should be maintained and available for review

Any problem areas found as a result of such investigations must be explained and/or resolved

Documented evidence of actions taken to resolve actual or apparent adverse impact should be maintained and available for review.

An IRA must be conducted at least once each year

KEY OBSERVATIONS – Compensation Systems

Discrepancies identified by the analysis should be discussed with other members of management to determine appropriate corrective action.

The OFCCP may take a comparable worth approach to its review of a company's wages and salaries.

A comparable worth approach to compensation analysis seeks to compare jobs whose jobs duties are not equal but are of equal **value** to the employer, for example, all jobs in the same labor grade.

The OFCCP may make the assumption that jobs placed into the same labor grades are jobs that are of equal **value** to the employer.

Comparable worth is not required by law. It is different than equal pay.

The OFCCP may attempt to make generalizations about job responsibilities being identical by virtue of same job title or salary grade.

The OFCCP may assume that if two job titles are in the same salary grade or range, then they are equal for purposes of pay equity analysis.

Ensure that the salaries and total compensation for disabled individuals and covered veterans are on par with other employees and that any discrimination does not exist due to disability or veteran status.

CHECKLIST: JAAR Disparities – Action-Oriented Programs

Review each area of concentration or under-representation identified by the analysis and prepare a written explanation for each occurrence and file it in the affirmative action file.

WHERE A CONCENTRATION OF PROTECTED CLASSES EXIST:

❏ Attempt to provide promotion and transfer opportunities out of the segment.

❏ Utilize a promotional review procedure targeting departments that have a concentration of protected class members.

❏ Notify department/segment management of concentration status.

❏ Review the personnel files of the protected class members in the related departments in order to develop career path opportunities elsewhere in the workforce.

WHERE AN UNDER-REPRESENTATION OF PROTECTED CLASSES EXIST:

❏ Notify department/segment management of under-representation status.

❏ As placement opportunities into the segment occur, consider under-representation status.

❏ Review the personnel files of the protected class members in the related departments in order to develop career path opportunities elsewhere in the workforce.

CHECKLIST: Utilization Analysis –
Action-Oriented Programs

❏ Expand recruitment advertisement media to include more publications representing minority and female interests and web sites for minority and female professional associations.

❏ Place employment advertisements in minority and female trade and association journals or other publications.

❏ Attend job fairs, and/or trade shows targeting minorities and females.

❏ Increase college-recruiting programs, where appropriate, to include institutions that have a high representation of minorities and females.

❏ Develop and utilize consistent employment selection procedures.

❏ Train all employees involved in the recruitment process to conduct interviews in a lawful manner and to refer applicants in a nondiscriminatory fashion, stressing the importance of assessing candidates against job requirements.

❏ Inform recruiting sources verbally, and in writing, of the Company's commitment to EEO and affirmative action, stipulating that these sources actively recruit and refer minorities and females for all positions listed without regard to race, sex, creed, color, age, veteran status, disability, religion or national origin.

❏ Require a written nondiscrimination and affirmative action statement of commitment from all temporary employment and recruiting agencies with which the Company lists open positions.

❏   Inform secondary schools and colleges and/or vocational/technical institutions, especially those with predominantly minority and female enrollments, of the Company's affirmative action policy in writing.

❏   Host meetings for professional associations that represent minorities and females.

❏   Establish meaningful contacts and working relationships with community agencies and/or organizations and recruiting sources that support minorities and females.

❏   Develop and utilize a management trainee and/or mentoring program in order to improve protected class representation in the top management job groups. (i.e. internships, job shadowing)

See also *"Checklist: Impact Ratio Analysis Disparities"* for Hires and Promotions.

CHECKLIST: Impact Ratio Analysis Disparities – Action-Oriented Programs

The following items represent suggested good faith efforts, some of which may not be applicable.

ADVERSE IMPACT – HIRES:

❑ Require Human Resources and/or Senior Management review and approval of all hires to ensure compliance with established Company guidelines.

❑ Recruit at secondary schools and colleges and/or vocational/technical institutions, especially those with predominantly minority and female enrollments.

❑ Post open positions on appropriate web sites for secondary schools and colleges especially those with predominant minority and female enrollments. (i.e. college placement web sites, career centers)

❑ Post open positions on appropriate web sites for minority and female professional associations.

❑ Place employment advertising in appropriate female and/or minority trade and association journals or other publications and media.

❑ Participate in job fairs targeting females and/or minorities.

❑ Develop and utilize an employee referral system, encouraging all employees to participate.

❑ Distribute job descriptions to all recruiting sources involved in the selection process.

❑ Maintain and utilize a retrieval file of qualified female and/or minority applicants.

❏ Send open position notifications to community agencies that support minorities and females, focusing on those job groups that are underutilized or indicated potential adverse impact.

ADVERSE IMPACT – PROMOTIONS:

❏ Require Human Resources and/or Senior Management approval for all promotions.

❏ Develop and utilize formal career counseling for employees.

❏ Ensure Company sponsored training programs are consistently available to all employees and encourage female and minority employees to participate.

❏ Consistently post promotional and/or transfer opportunities. (i.e. intranet system and Company web site)

❏ Review all pertinent employment records when making competitive promotion selections.

❏ Require management personnel to submit written justification when apparently qualified minority or female employees are passed over for advancement.

ADVERSE IMPACT – TERMINATIONS:

❏ Require Human Resources and/or Senior Management approval for all terminations.

❏ Develop and utilize a progressive discipline policy for the resolution of employee conduct issues.

❏ Develop and utilize performance management standards for the resolution of employer job performance issues.

❏ Develop and consistently utilize a termination policy for all terminations.

❏ Develop and utilize "witnessed counseling" and termination sessions.

❏ Conduct training for management staff involved in discipline and performance management to eliminate the potential for bias.

❏ Conduct exit interviews on a consistent basis.

❏ Utilize a third party to conduct exit interviews to ensure impartial findings.

❏ Conduct post termination interviews after a specified period of time in order to isolate any problematic issues.

ADVERSE IMPACT – LAYOFFS/REDUCTIONS IN FORCE:

❏ Require Human Resources and/or Senior Management review and approval of all layoffs/reductions in force.

❏ Develop and consistently utilize a layoff/reduction in force policy when such actions occur.

❏ Ensure only valid, job-related criteria is used in layoff/reduction in force selection decisions.

❏ Conduct adverse impact analyses prior to a layoff/reduction in force.

CHECKLIST: Compensation Systems
Disparities – Action-Oriented Programs

❑ Require Human Resources and/or Senior Management review and approval of all job offers to ensure compliance with established compensation guidelines.

❑ Develop and consistently utilize salary ranges to ensure equity in position salaries.

❑ Review exempt/non-exempt designations to ensure full compliance with ESA regulations.

❑ Conduct periodic pay equity analyses.

❑ Determine salary adjustments through a process that includes measurable components. (i.e. position descriptions, market surveys, COLA)

❑ Develop and consistently utilize formal performance evaluation and merit increase program.

❑ Train all management personnel on the performance evaluation process and compensation system.

❑ Determine if all employees are being paid at least at the minimum of their respective salary ranges. If not, determine if a business-related reason exists for paying below the minimum.

❑ Review the job compensation system to determine if it is based on valid job content and other business-related criteria.

❏ Document, maintain, and make available for review evidence of job responsibilities (e.g. job descriptions) to support differences of the type of work performed among incumbents in similar titles (i.e. an Accounting Manager vs. a Human Resource Manager vs. an Information Technology Manager vs. a Warehouse Manager.)

❏ Document, maintain, and make available for review evidence of job responsibilities (e.g. job descriptions) to support differences among varying jobs in the same salary range.

STEP 4 – CONDUCTING THE QUALITATIVE ANALYSES

41 CFR§60-2.17(b)(4) SELECTION, RECRUITMENT, REFERRAL, AND OTHER PERSONNEL PROCEDURES

As part of the in-depth analyses of the total employment an assessment of selection, recruitment, referral, and other personnel procedures must be conducted to determine whether they result in disparities in the employment or advancement of minorities or women; and any other areas that might impact the success of the affirmative action program. Think of this as an audit of all of the human resource practices to ensure fairness in the company's practices.

The key observations contained in this section may be used to assist in evaluating and auditing the company's overall employment processes. Documentation should be maintained to the extent necessary to demonstrate consistent employment practices.

Remember that the affirmative action program is a process. As such, the OFCCP expects that all HR and employment-related programs will be evaluated on a continual basis.

41 CFR§60-2.17(d) INTERNAL AUDIT & REPORTING SYSTEM

Companies are required to develop and implement an auditing system that periodically measures the effectiveness of the affirmative action program. The internal audit and reporting system should incorporate the following actions:

- A process for monitoring personnel activity
- Scheduled internal reporting
- Scheduled management review of report results
- A procedure and/or practice for advising management of program effectiveness and making recommendations for program improvement

A checklist for internal audit and reporting is included in this section.

Accomplishments of Prior Year Goals Report

While not specifically required in the regulations, an analysis of the progress or accomplishments of the goals set in the prior year affirmative action plan should be conducted. A report documenting this analysis will be requested during a compliance evaluation. In addition, if the company receives a compliance check, this report must be shown to the compliance officer as evidence that there is a current affirmative action plan in place. This report should be prepared each year when the plan is prepared.

This report is a valuable tool in assessing the effectiveness of an Affirmative Action Program as required in CFR §60-2.17(d)(2). The report must indicate:

- Which job groups were underutilized in the prior year
- The placement rate goal for each underutilized job group
- The number of placements (hires and promotions) into the underutilized job group in order to determine the placement rate that was achieved
- For those job groups in which the goal was not met, a description of the good faith efforts undertaken to achieve the goal

While preparing the report is the first step, using the results as an analytical tool is important. It is important to understand how the jobs in the underutilized job groups were filled during the prior year — by hires or by promotions – and then determine the reasons why placement rate goals were not met and possible underlying causes.

KEY OBSERVATIONS – Evaluation of Selection, Recruitment, Referral, and Other Personnel Procedures

RECRUITING AND SELECTION PROCESS:

Are job descriptions in place? If so, are they accurate?

If job descriptions are not in place, is there a process to document job requirements and specifications such as a requisition form or other document?

Does the Human Resources department review job descriptions and/ or documentation with line managers to ensure that they contain valid, job-related criteria?

Are requisitions used in the hiring process? Does the Human Resources department review them?

If requisitions are not in place, is there a consistent process that drives the recruitment and selection process?

If external agencies are used in the sourcing and recruiting process, are they advised of the company's Equal Employment Opportunity and Affirmative Action obligations and required to adhere to them?

Are external agencies notified to attract and refer a slate of candidates that are representative of the availability of qualified minorities and females?

Are managers involved in the sourcing and recruiting process? If so, do they receive adequate instruction and training on Equal Employment Opportunity/Affirmative Action obligations?

Who maintains applicant flow? Are these individuals/agencies provided with adequate instruction and training on Equal Employment Opportunity/Affirmative Action implications?

Are there employee referral systems or processes in place? If so, how are they communicated to the employees?

Are employee referral systems monitored to ensure against adverse impact?

Are managers trained in lawful interview techniques?

Are tests used during the selection process? If so, are they validated? Are they job-related?

Are all steps of the selection process reviewed for adverse impact?

Are all steps of the selection process (e.g. interviews, assessments, and tests) documented?

Can the reasons for not selecting minority or female candidates be justified or explained?

Are reasons for selection and rejection documented?

JOB OFFERS & HIRES:

Does the Human Resources department review all job offers? If so, what is the extent of that review (e.g. appropriateness of skills with respect to incumbents; salary review with respect to incumbents)?

Does the Human Resources department extend all job offers?

Are all job offers extended in writing?

Are the reasons for declined job offers documented?

PROMOTIONS & INTERNAL PLACEMENTS:

Is there a process for open positions to be posted or communicated internally?

If there is such a process, are employees aware of how to access these postings?

If no such process exists, how do employees become aware of advancement opportunities?

Does the Human Resources department review all promotions?

Are valid, job-related criteria used in the selection of internal candidates?

Can the reasons for not selecting minority or female candidates be justified or explained?

Is written documentation or justification maintained regarding each promotion decision?

TRAINING & DEVELOPMENT:

Is any specific, periodic, in-house training conducted?

How are employees made aware of such programs?

How are employees selected to attend such training programs?

Is access to these programs monitored to ensure against adverse impact?

Do all employees have equal access to training opportunities?

Do all employees have equal access to development programs such as educational assistance and support for membership in professional organizations?

Are records maintained regarding attendance at training programs and participation in development programs?

COMPENSATION:

Are job descriptions in place? If so, are they accurate and up-to-date?

If job descriptions are not in place, is there a process to document job requirements and specifications?

Are all employees appropriately classified as exempt or non-exempt in accordance with the Fair Labor Standards Act guidelines?

Is the system that measures relative worth of positions still in line with the needs and culture of the organization?

Do pay levels ensure equality and equity for those employees in jobs requiring similar experience, knowledge, skills, and abilities?

Has a review of increases granted to employees in protected classes been completed to ensure discrimination is not occurring?

Are all forms of compensation appropriate, effective, and linked to the company's mission and goals?

Does the company have a clear and effective compensation policy to ensure consistency of pay actions and pay decisions?

Has a formal audit of the company's compensation program and systems been conducted to ensure that there is no discrimination against minorities and females?

Are the results documented?

Have problem areas been addressed?

Does the Human Resources department provide guidance to managers in the proper application of the compensation program?

Is the Human Resources department consulted with respect to compensation decisions?

If labor grades, salary grades, or broad banding is used in the compensation systems, can differences in pay be justified using nondiscriminatory factors?

Does the company have broad-based job formulas where incumbents have responsibility across a wide array of functions? (i.e. Manager of a clerical staff vs. warehouse staff vs. scientists or engineers) If so, can their differences be differentiated through documented evidence?

PERFORMANCE MANAGEMENT:

Are the performance appraisal systems monitored by the Human Resources department?

Do managers receive appropriate training regarding the company's appraisal policy and systems?

Are managers trained in the appropriate way to document performance issues (both positive and negative issues)?

Is there a written performance appraisal system?

Are appraisal systems applied consistently?

Does the performance appraisal system evaluate the performance of managers with respect to EEO matters?

Are employees trained in the performance management process?

Do employees have an opportunity to meet with their managers for formal discussions?

How often is a formal performance management review conducted?

Are performance reviews used in compensation decisions?

TERMINATIONS:

Does the Human Resources department review all terminations?

Are managers aware of the policy for progressive discipline? Do they receive adequate training in the process?

Are managers aware of the policy or process for performance improvement? Do they receive adequate training?

Are layoffs conducted according to policy and are they documented?

Do managers receive training on the layoff policy and the appropriate selection of individuals for layoff?

Is adverse impact conducted when a layoff takes place?

Does the Human Resources department or management conduct an exit interview? If so, is it documented?

Is a letter of resignation requested from those who voluntarily resign?

Does the Human Resources department record each termination by reason?

KEY OBSERVATIONS – Evaluation of Accomplishments of Prior Year Goals

If jobs were filled primarily by external hires, then examine:

Applicant flow to see if a sufficient number of applicants were provided

Recruitment sources to see if they align with the types of jobs for which they are recruiting

Level of commitment (and involvement) in establishing relationships with recruitment sources (e.g. mailing job listings to community organizations or inviting community organization to visit facility).

Success with prior year commitments (action-oriented programs). Did they provide a sufficient number of quality candidates? What actions can be taken to influence or strengthen their success?

Whether offers made to minorities and females were rejected. If this is the case, the reasons for the rejections should be examined.

Whether adverse impact exists for job groups in which goals were set.

If jobs were filled primarily by internal placements, especially promotions, then examine:

Minority and females in feeder groups to determine if there was a sufficient internal pool from which to select.

Prior year commitments (action-oriented programs) with respect to the promotion process. For example, conducting skills inventories to identify promotable females and minorities or increasing promotability through training and job rotations programs.

Whether adverse impact exists for job groups in which goals were set.

The types of promotions (or other movements), to ensure that all job changes have been appropriately identified and classified.

In conducting an overall analysis, it is important to understand why goals have not been met for each job group. The following should be examined:

The degree of underutilization (e.g. 10% incumbency vs. 30% availability) and whether efforts are aligned accordingly.

The history of underutilization in each job group (e.g. has it been underutilized for the past three years?).

Whether there were any substantial changes during the year such as reorganizations, layoffs, large contract awards, and the impact of these changes on the workforce and the affirmative action goals.

Whether there are particular or unique requirements (e.g. extensive travel, weekend or night shifts) that might hamper attempts to attract qualified minorities or females.

Whether any of the positions that were filled in the job group had specific and unique requirements that limited the applicant pool for that specific opening.

CHECKLIST: Internal Audit & Reporting –
41 CFR§60-2.17(d)

Internal auditing systems are required to be in place so that the company's employment practices and the effectiveness of the total affirmative action program can be monitored. The requirements for an effective internal audit and reporting system include:

❏   Maintain I-9s properly.

  • I-9s should be kept separate from employee's file
  • I-9s should be periodically audited for accuracy
  • I-9s should be maintained in accordance with governing laws and regulations of the Immigration and Naturalization Service (INS)

❏   Provide managers periodic updates with respect to affirmative action progress.

❏   Retain all employment records for at least two (2) years from the date of the creation of the record or the personnel action involved. Note: For companies with fewer than 150 employees or less than $150,000 in government contracts, the retention period is one (1) year.

❏   Maintain and monitor applicant flow by job group identifying applicants for employment, and when possible, by gender and race.

❏   Maintain and monitor records of new hires identifying each person by name, hire date, job classification, department, gender, and race.

❏   Maintain and monitor records of transfers and promotions identifying each individual by name, transfer/promotion date, job classification (old and new), department number (old and new), gender, and race.

❑ Maintain and monitor records of terminations identifying each individual by name, termination date, job classification, department, gender, race, and reason for termination.

❑ Maintain reports of education and training activities in which each employee has participated.

STEP 5 – DEVELOPING A PROGRAM FOR INDIVIDUALS WITH DISABILITIES AND COVERED VETERANS

INTRODUCTION

(41 CFR§250 & 41 CFR§741)

In addition to the affirmative action plan and program for minorities and females, there is a separate set of requirements and regulations governing nondiscrimination and affirmative action for Individuals with Disabilities, Disabled Veterans, Veterans of the Vietnam Era, and other categories of protected veterans (collectively referred to in this section as "covered veterans.") Normally, a single plan is prepared covering these requirements because they are quite similar under the governing laws and regulations, namely the Rehabilitation Act of 1973 and Vietnam Era Veterans' Readjustment Assistance Act of 1974, as amended.

The regulations specify certain actions that must be taken as well as describe the required contents of affirmative action programs. Unlike the requirements for the minorities and females program, the governing regulations for the disabled and veterans programs contain no quantitative analysis.

Required Actions

AVAILABILITY OF THE PLAN FOR INSPECTION: 41 CFR§60-250.41 & 41 CFR§60.741.41

A company's Veterans & Disabled Affirmative Action Plan must be available for inspection, upon request, by any employee or applicant. This does not apply to the Minorities and Female plan and it is recommended that the plan that is developed for Minorities and Females **should not** be available for inspection.

In addition, the hours during which the plan is available for inspection should be publicized.

INVITATION TO SELF-IDENTIFY:
41 CFR§60-250.42 & 41 CFR§60.741.42

A company must invite "post-offer" applicants and employees to inform the company if they believe that they may be covered by the Rehabilitation Act and wish to benefit under the affirmative action program. The Americans with Disabilities Act specifies that this invitation to self-identify can be extended to applicants only after an offer of employment has been made.

The post-offer Invitation to Self-Identify can be accomplished through a posting or other appropriate employee communication. The communication can advise that the affirmative action plan is available for inspection upon request and include the location and hours during which the plan may be reviewed.

MANDATORY JOB LISTINGS

All full-time and part-time employment openings must be listed with the local/state employment service or with America's Job Bank, with the exception of: a) executive and top management positions, b) positions that will be filled from within the company, and c) temporary positions lasting three (3) days or less.

Required Contents of Affirmative Action Programs

EQUAL EMPLOYMENT OPPORTUNITY POLICY STATEMENT:
41 CFR§60-250.44(A) & 41 CFR§60.741.44(A)

Government contractors are required to have an EEO policy. The policy statement must be included in the affirmative action plan and posted "on company bulletin boards." All applicants and employees with disabilities must be made aware of the contents of the policy. To accomplish this, reasonable accommodations may be required such as reading the policy to an individual with a visual impairment.

REVIEW OF PERSONNEL PROCESSES:
41 CFR§60-250.44(B) & 41 CFR§60.741.44(B)

Personnel processes must be reviewed and modified, if necessary, to ensure systematic consideration of the job qualifications of applicants and employees with known disabilities and covered veterans for job vacancies filled either by hiring or promotion, and for all training opportunities offered or available.

PHYSICAL & MENTAL QUALIFICATIONS:
41 CFR§60-250.44(C) & 41 CFR§60.741.44(C)

All physical and mental qualification requirements of positions must be reviewed and modified, if necessary, to ensure that they are job-related and consistent with business necessity, and do not screen out, or tend to screen out, qualified individuals with disabilities or covered veterans. Examples of physical qualifications are lifting, standing, bending, etc. Examples of mental qualifications are education, experience, etc.

REASONABLE ACCOMMODATIONS:
41 CFR§60-250.44(D) & 41 CFR§60.741.44(D)

Reasonable accommodations must be made for the known physical or mental limitations of otherwise qualified individuals with disabilities and disabled veterans.

HARASSMENT:
41 CFR§60-250.44(E) & 41 CFR§60.741.44(E)

Procedures must be developed and implemented to ensure that individuals with disabilities and covered veterans are not harassed because of their disability or veteran status.

OUTREACH PROGRAM & POSITIVE RECRUITMENT:
41 CFR§60-250.44(F) & 41 CFR§60.741.44(F)

A company must engage in outreach and positive recruitment activities that are reasonably designed to effectively recruit individuals with disabilities and covered veterans.

DISSEMINATION OF POLICY:
41 CFR§60-250.44(G) & 41 CFR§60.741.44(G)

Procedures must be developed to communicate both internally and externally the obligation to engage in affirmative action efforts to employ and advance in employment qualified individuals with disabilities and covered veterans.

INTERNAL AUDIT & REPORTING SYSTEM:
41 CFR§60-250.44(H) & 41 CFR§60.741.44(H)

An internal audit and reporting system must be developed that will measure the effectiveness of the affirmative action program and compliance with specific obligations.

RESPONSIBILITY FOR IMPLEMENTATION:
41 CFR§60-250.44(I) & 41 CFR§60.741.44(I)

A company official must be named and identified as the individual in the company who has been assigned responsibility for the company's affirmative action activity.

Note: Refer to the discussion and checklist regarding Responsibility for Implementation contained in Step 2 (41 CFR§60-2.17(a) DESIGNATION OF RESPONSIBILITY.)

TRAINING:
41 CFR§60-250.44(J) & 41 CFR§60.741.44(J)

All personnel involved in the recruitment, screening, selection, promotion, disciplinary, and related processes must be trained to ensure that commitments specified in the Affirmative Action Plan are implemented.

CHECKLIST: Disabled & Veterans Affirmative Action Program

The following checklist is provided to assist in ensuring that the program and plan contain all the required actions and elements. In the event of an OFCCP Compliance Evaluation, the presence of documentation is necessary proof of meeting the obligations listed.

AVAILABILITY OF THE PLAN FOR INSPECTION:

❏ The Veterans & Disabled Affirmative Action Plan is available for inspection.

❏ The hours during which the plan is available for inspection is publicized to all employees and applicants.

INVITATION TO SELF-IDENTIFY:

❏ The Invitation to Self-Identify is extended after an offer of employment is made but before job duties commence.

❏ Current employees are advised that they can self-identify their disabled or veteran status after employment begins.

❏ There is an appropriate process in place to allow employees to self-identify their disabled or veteran status.

MANDATORY JOB LISTINGS:

❏ All full-time and part-time employment openings are listed with the local/state employment service or with America's Job Bank, with the exception of: a) executive and top management positions, b) positions that will be filled from within the company, and c) temporary positions lasting three (3) days or less.

EEO POLICY STATEMENT:

❏ The EEO policy statement confirms that the company does not discriminate against individuals with physical or mental disabilities, disabled veterans, veterans of the Vietnam era, and other categories of covered veterans in all areas of employment.

❏ The EEO policy states that the company will provide equal employment opportunity and affirmative action for such individuals.

❏ The policy statement is posted on company bulletin boards and is communicated internally through other media such as a company Intranet.

❏ All applicants and employees with disabilities are informed of the contents of the policy.

❏ The company must ensure that the contents of the policy are available to all applicants and employees with disabilities.

REVIEW OF PERSONNEL PROCESSES:

❏ Applicants are reviewed against job-related qualifications.

❏ Qualified applicants are not denied access to available positions because of their disability or veteran status.

❏ Applicants with known disabilities and known covered veterans are considered for all open positions for which they may be qualified when the position(s) applied for is unavailable.

❏ All employees and prospective employees are informed of the company's commitment to affirmative action to increase employment opportunities for qualified individuals with disabilities and qualified covered veterans.

❏ Employees are not limited or barred from promotional opportunities because of their disability or veteran status.

❏ Employees are not limited or barred from training opportunities because of their disability or veteran status.

❏ Workplace accessibility is reviewed periodically to ensure that applicants and employees in wheelchairs have access to all the applicant and Human Resources areas.

❏ A periodic review of positions physical and mental qualifications must be conducted for each position to ensure that the qualifications for all positions are job-related and consistent with business necessity.

❏ Positions are reviewed as openings occur.

❏ All new positions are reviewed.

❏ Documentation on the results of each review is maintained.

REASONABLE ACCOMMODATION:

❏ Reasonable accommodation is made during the interview process as well as throughout an individual's period of employment to ensure access to promotional opportunities, training, and other work-related events and activities.

❏ Employees are informed that they may request a reasonable accommodation at any time.

❏ A process is in place to review all requests for reasonable accommodation and each request for a reasonable accommodation is documented.

❏ Appropriate documentation is made and retained for all requests for reasonable accommodation.

INTERNAL AUDIT & MONITORING:
❏   The Reasonable Accommodation process is periodically audited and is communicated to all employees.

❏   Records are maintained of all requests for Reasonable Accommodation.

❏   Records regarding accommodation requests are maintained separately from the employee file.

❏   The Invitation to Self-Identify documents are maintained separately from the employee file.

HARASSMENT:
❏   The company's harassment policy includes harassment on the basis of disability or veteran status.

❏   There is a process in place to investigate harassment.

❏   The harassment policy and the complaint resolution process are communicated to all employees.

TRAINING:
❏   Managers and others involved with the hiring process receive training and other information on issues specific to reasonable accommodation for disabilities, essential job functions, and interviewing individuals with disabilities.

INTERNAL DISSEMINATION OF POLICY OUTREACH AND POSITIVE RECRUITMENT:

(The OFCCP does not "contemplate that contractors will necessarily undertake all the activities listed.")

❏ Include all pertinent policies in the Employee Handbook (i.e. EEO, Affirmative Action, Harassment, Leave of Absence.)

❏ Include all pertinent policies in the Company Policy Manual (i.e. EEO, Affirmative Action, Harassment, Leave of Absence.)

❏ Periodically inform all employees and prospective employees of the Company's commitment to EEO/Affirmative Action (i.e. posting the EEO policy, payroll stuffers, operational training programs, etc.)

❏ Schedule meetings with all employees to discuss the Company's policies and commitment to EEO/Affirmative Action and explain individual employee responsibilities (i.e. EEO, Affirmative Action, Harassment, Leave of Absence.)

❏ Publicize pertinent policies in Company publications (i.e. newsletter, intranet, Company web site, annual report, etc.).

❏ Notify employees of the name and phone number of the EEO Official/Officer/Coordinator.

❏ Notify executive, management, and supervisory personnel of the intent of affirmative action and the individual responsibility for effective implementation, making clear the Company's attitude (i.e. scheduled meetings, periodic correspondence directed to appropriate individuals, etc. Document all meetings with minutes that include a list of attendees.)

❏ Discuss the Company's policies and commitments in new hire orientation programs (i.e. EEO, Affirmative Action, Harassment, Leave of Absence.)

❑ Discuss the Company's policies and commitments in management training programs (i.e. EEO, Affirmative Action, Harassment, Leave of Absence.)

❑ Meet with union officials and/or employee representatives to inform them of the Company's policy and request their cooperation.

❑ Include articles on the accomplishments of individuals with disabilities and covered veterans in Company publications.

❑ Include individuals with disabilities and covered veterans when employees are featured in internal Company publications (i.e. newsletters, employee handbook, training manuals, intranet, Company web site, etc.)

EXTERNAL DISSEMINATION OF POLICY OUTREACH AND POSITIVE RECRUITMENT:
(The OFCCP does not "contemplate that contractors will necessarily undertake all the activities listed.")

❑ Enlist assistance and support of specialized recruiting sources to provide meaningful employment opportunities to qualified individuals with disabilities and qualified covered veterans.

❑ Establish meaningful contacts with appropriate social service agencies, organizations of and for individuals with disabilities and covered veterans, and vocational rehabilitation agencies or facilities for such purposes as advice, technical assistance and referral of potential employees.

(Note: These recruiting sources and agencies can include State employment service, education and vocational rehabilitation agencies, sheltered workshops, college placement offices, the local veterans' employment representative in the local employment service office, Department of Veterans Affairs regional office, veterans' counselors on college campuses and local veterans groups and veterans service centers.)

❏ Inform all recruiting sources, including placement firms and schools and colleges, and other social service agencies, verbally and in writing, of the Company's commitment to EEO and affirmative action.

❏ Inform union officials and/or employee representatives of the company's policy and request their cooperation.

❏ Participate in job fairs and career days that focus on U.S. Veterans and individuals with disabilities.

❏ Advertise job openings in publications and media targeted at U.S. Veterans and individuals with disabilities.

❏ Conduct formal briefing sessions with representatives from specials recruiting sources including: plant tours, clear and concise explanations of current and future job openings, position descriptions, worker specifications and explanations of Company's selection process. Make formal arrangements for referral of applicant follow-up with sources and feedback on disposition of applicants.

❏ Incorporate special efforts to reach individuals with disabilities and covered veterans when recruiting at schools and educations institutions.

❏ Participate in work-study programs with rehabilitation facilities and schools which specialize in training or educating individuals with disabilities and/or covered veterans.

❏ Include individuals with disabilities when employees are featured in external Company publications (i.e. consumer, promotional, or employment advertising.)

❏ Make available individuals with disabilities and covered veterans for participation in career days, youth motivation programs, and related activities in their communities.

❏   Utilize local chapters of organizations of and for individuals with disabilities and covered veterans to attract individuals who have the requisite skills and can be recruited through affirmative action measures.

❏   Consider applicants who are known to be disabled or a covered veteran for all positions for which they may be qualified when the position applied for is unavailable.

APPENDIX A

DEFINITIONS AND TERMS

Ability
Aptitude or competence, the skill or proficiency needed to perform certain tasks.

Accessibility
The extent to which a contractor's or employer's facility is readily approachable and does not inhibit the mobility of individuals with disabilities, particularly such areas as the personnel office, worksite, and public areas.

Adverse Impact
Practices or policies, which result in the selection of members of a protected class at a rate lower than that of other groups. Enforcement agencies look for a selection rate for a race, sex, or ethnic group which is less than four-fifths (80%) of the group with the highest rate as evidence of adverse impact.

Affected Class
Groups of employees, former employees, or applicants who have experienced and/or continue to experience the loss of employment opportunities or benefits due to discriminatory practices or policies of the employer.

Affirmative Action (AA)
Actions, policies, and procedures undertaken by a contractor in recruiting, hiring, promoting, and all other personnel actions that are designed to achieve equal employment opportunity and eliminate the present effects of past discrimination. Affirmative action requires: (1) thorough, systematic efforts to prevent discrimination from occurring or to detect and eliminate it as promptly as possible; and (2) recruitment and outreach measures.

Affirmative Action Clauses

The clauses set forth in 41 CFR§§60-250.4 and 60-741.4 that must be included in federal contracts and subcontracts of $10,000 and over. These two clauses outline the affirmative action requirements for special disabled veterans, Vietnam-era veterans (41 CFR§60-250.4), and individuals with disabilities (41 CFR§60-741.4). These clauses are a part of covered contracts regardless of whether they are physically incorporated into the contract and whether the contract is written.

Affirmative Action Plan (AAP)

A written set of specific, results-oriented procedures to be followed by all federal contractors holding contracts of $50,000 or more and employing 50 or more people and intended to remedy the effects of past discrimination against or under-utilization of women and minorities. The effectiveness of the plan is measured by the results it actually achieves rather than by the results intended and by the good faith efforts undertaken by the contractor to increase the pool of qualified women and minorities in all parts of the organization.

Age Discrimination in Employment Act (ADEA)

ADEA is a federal law that prohibits discrimination on the basis of age by employers of 20 or more employees against people over 40. Where age is a bona fide occupational qualification, or where the person is in a certain key executive or policy-making position and will have a pension in excess of $40,000 per year, the law exempts them from coverage. These employees may be required to retire at age 65.

American Indian or Alaskan Native

A person with origins in any of the original peoples of North America who maintains cultural identification through tribal affiliation or has community recognition as an American Indian or Alaskan Native.

Annual Goal

An annual target for the placement of underutilized groups of protected class members in job groups where under-utilization exists. (See also Placement Rate Goal)

Applicant
An applicant is anyone who expresses an interest in employment (by resume, employment application, e-mail, web site, job fair, etc.), if considered by a company hiring authority for a job opening or specific position. Note: also consider adding—"and who meets the minimum qualifications for the position under consideration." Where the applicant does not specify race/ethnic group and/or gender, a good faith effort is required to identify this information. Employment applications must be retained for the longer of: two years or two AAP years (both current and prior AAP years).

Applicant Flow
The number of people who apply for employment for a job title over a certain period of time, sorted and analyzed by gender and race.

Applicant Flow Log
A chronological listing (e.g. electronic file, manual list) which records each applicant who applies for employment or promotion. Data includes applicant's name, race, national origin, gender, referral source, date of application, job title applied for, and disposition.

Applicant Pool
All of the people who have applied for particular jobs over a period of time who form the collection of candidates from which selection decisions are made.

Apprentice
A worker who is employed to learn a skilled trade in a structural program of on-the-job training and related instruction.

Asian-Pacific Islander
A person with origins in any of the original peoples of the Far East, Southeast Asia, the Indian subcontinent, or the Pacific Islands. This area includes, for example, China, Japan, Korea, the Philippine Republic, and Samoa; and, on the Indian subcontinent, includes India, Pakistan, Bangladesh, Sri Lanka, Nepal, Sikkim, and Bhutan.

Availability

The availability of minorities or women for a job group means the percentage of minorities or women among persons in the relevant labor area and/or internal feeder pools having the requisite qualifications to perform the positions included in the job group. The term is broad enough to include any factor that is in fact relevant to determining the availability of individuals for the jobs in the job group. Availability figures are used in determining whether under-utilization exists and, where a goal is established, in determining the level of the goal. In determining availability for a job group, a contractor must consider at least the two factors specified in 21 CFR§2.14 (c).

Black (or African-American)

An individual, not of Hispanic origin, with origins in any of the black racial groups of Africa.

Bona Fide Occupational Qualification (BFOQ)

A defense allowing an employer to limit a particular job to members of one sex, religion, or national origin group. The courts have held that the statutory BFOQ provision in Title VII is a very narrow exception to the general prohibition against discrimination on the basis of those characteristics. In enforcing the Executive Order, OFCCP follows Title VII principles regarding the BFOQ exception. An employer claiming that sex is a BFOQ for a job has to show that all (or substantially all) members of the excluded sex are incapable of performing the duties of the job and that failure to allow the exclusion would undermine the "essence" - the central purpose or mission - of the employer's business. Race can never be considered a BFOQ for a job.

Business Necessity

A defense available when the employer has a criterion for selection that is facially neutral but which excludes members of one sex, race, national origin, or religious group at a substantially higher rate than members of other groups, thus creating adverse impact. The employer must be able to prove that the challenged practices effectively carry out the business purposes they are alleged to serve and that no alternative, nondiscriminatory practices can achieve the safe and efficient operation of its business.

Civil Rights Act of 1964

Civil Rights Act of 1964 is a comprehensive federal law which makes it illegal to discriminate on the basis of race, color, religion, sex, and national origin. Title VII of the law was the first to specifically ban discrimination in the employment setting and is enforced by the Equal Employment Opportunity Commission (EEOC).

Class Action

A court action on behalf of an affected class alleging an unlawful pattern of discrimination against a group that shares similar characteristics (age, race, etc.). An individual, a group, and/or a government agency can bring a class action suit.

Cohort Analysis

A comparison of the treatment of similarly situated individuals or groups.

Complaint

A written charge filed with OFCCP by an employee, former employee, applicant for employment, or by a third party alleging specific violations of Executive Order 11246, Section 503 or 38 U.S.C.§4212.

Compliance

Meeting the requirements and obligations of affirmative action imposed by Executive Order 11246, Section 503 of the Rehabilitation Act, Section 4212 of the Vietnam Era Veterans' Readjustment Assistance Act and their implementing regulations.

Compliance Officer

An employee of the OFCCP engaged in the investigation of employment discrimination charges and conducting compliance evaluations. The former name for this position was Equal Opportunity Specialist (EOS).

Conciliation Agreement

A binding written agreement between a contractor and OFCCP that details specific contractor commitments to resolve major or substantive violations of Executive Order 11246, the Rehabilitation Act, or the Vietnam Era Veterans' Readjustment Assistance Act.

Contracting Agency
For purposes of Executive Order 11246, Section 503 and 38 U.S.C.§4212, a contracting agency is any department, agency, establishment, or instrumentality of the United States (under the Executive Order, limited to the executive branch of the Government), including any wholly owned Government corporation, which enters into contracts. See 41 CFR §60-1.3, §60-250.2, and §60-741.2.

Contractor
A Contractor is a firm which does business with the federal government. A prime contractor is one who receives $50,000 or more in contracts each year and employs more than 50 people in total employment. A subcontractor is a firm that performs part of the contract at the direction of the prime contractor and receives $10,000 or more in subcontracts each year.

Corrective Action
Correction of deficiencies identified during a compliance evaluation of an affirmative action plan.

Declination
a) A documented offer of employment or promotion refused by an individual after being offered a specific position at a specific rate of pay. (Listed by gender, ethnic, and racial group.)
b) A documented offer of a training course refused by an individual. (Listed by gender, ethnic, and racial group.)

Debarment
An order declaring a contractor ineligible for the award of future contracts or cancellation of current contracts. Debarment is one of the sanctions that can be imposed on a contractor who is found to be in violation of Executive Order 11246, Section 503 of the Rehabilitation Act or Section 4212 of the Vietnam Era Veterans' Readjustment Assistance Act.

Deficiency
Failure to fulfill a requirement of Executive Order 11246, Section 503 of the Rehabilitation Act or Section 4212 of the Vietnam Era Veterans' Readjustment Assistance Act, including implementing rules, regulations, and orders. "Deficiency" and "Violation" are often used interchangeably.

Department of Labor (DOL)
Administrative agency of the federal government charged with administering and enforcing employment laws.

Desk Audit
A review of a contractor's documents and materials to determine compliance with affirmative action practices and equal employment obligations as they relate to workforce structure, personnel policies and procedures, good faith efforts, and areas of potential discrimination. The Standard Compliance Review Report (SCRR) provides instructions for conducting a desk audit, which takes its name from the fact that this review and analysis is done at the desk of the Compliance Officer assigned to conduct the audit.

Disability
A Disability is a physical or mental impairment which substantially limits one or more major life activities, a record of having such an impairment, or being perceived as having such impairment.

Disabled Veteran
A person whose discharge or release from active duty was for a disability incurred or aggravated in the line of duty and who is entitled to a 30% or more disability payment under the regulations of the Veteran's Administration.

Discrimination
Illegal treatment of a person or group of persons based on race, sex, or other prohibited factor.

Disparate Impact
A theory or category of employment discrimination. Disparate impact discrimination can be found when a contractor's or employer's use of an otherwise neutral selection standard - such as a test, an interview, or a degree requirement - disqualifies members of a particular race or gender at a significantly higher rate than others and is not justified by business necessity or job-relatedness. An intent to discriminate is not necessary to this type of employment discrimination. The disparate impact theory can be used to analyze both objective and subjective selection standards.

79

Disparate Treatment

A theory or category of employment discrimination. Disparate treatment discrimination can be found when a contractor or employer treats an individual or group differently because of its race, color, religion, sex, national origin, disability, or veteran status. An intent to discriminate is a necessary element in this type of employment discrimination, which can be shown by direct evidence or inferred through statistical, anecdotal, and/or comparative evidence.

"Eighty Percent" Rule

Method of determining adverse impact. Selection rates for any group which are less than 80% (four-fifths) of the rate for other groups is evidence of a violation of this rule.

Employer

Under EEOC Policy Guidelines, a person or persons engaging in an industry affecting commerce who has 15 or more employees for each working day in each of the 20 or more weeks in the preceding year, or any agent thereof. Includes state and local governments, any federal agency subject to the provisions of Section 717 of the Civil Rights Act of 1964, as amended. Also includes any federal contractor or subcontractor or federally assisted construction contractor covered by Executive Order 11246, as amended.

Employer Information Report EEO-1

Also known as Standard Form 100, this annual report shows the representation of female and minority employees in an employer's total workforce as well as in standard job groupings (i.e., officials & managers, professionals, etc.). This report must be filed each year by any employer with 100 or more employees (50 or more for government contractors).

Employment Offer

An employer's offer to an applicant for employment, usually in a specified job. (Listed by gender, ethnic and racial group.)

Employment Practice

Any recruitment, hiring, selection practice, transfer or promotion policy, or any benefit provision or other function of the employer's employment process which operates as an analysis or screening device.

Enforcement
Administrative or judicial action to compel compliance with Executive Order 11246, Section 503 or 38 U.S.C.§4212 and their implementing regulations.

Equal Employment Opportunity
A system of employment practices under which individuals are not excluded from any participation, advancement, or benefits due to race, color, religion, sex, national origin, or any other action which cannot lawfully be the basis for employment actions.

Equal Employment Opportunity Commission (EEOC)
Established by Congress, the EEOC is made up of members appointed by the President and receives, processes, and investigates charges of employment discrimination under Title VII of the Civil Rights Act of 1964, Title I of the Americans with Disabilities Act, the Equal Pay Act of 1963, and the Age Discrimination in Employment Act of 1967. If the commission determines that there is reasonable cause to believe that the law has been violated, it first tries to obtain remedies for the affected individuals through conciliation and can bring suit in federal district court if conciliation efforts fail.

EEOC Guidelines
Interpretations of Title VII expressed by the EEOC that don't have the force of law, but tend to be supported by the courts. These positions are outlined in various EEOC publications ("Discrimination because of Religion", etc.).

Equal Opportunity Clause
The seven subparagraphs in Section 202 of Executive Order 11246, as amended. These paragraphs are required to be part of all contracts covered by the executive order.

Equal Opportunity Survey
This report will be sent to a substantial portion of all non-construction contractors each year. It requires them to provide to the OFCCP information regarding applicants, hires, promotions, terminations, compensation, and tenure by race and gender. Non-construction contracts can expect to receive and complete this report every other year.

EEO-1 Category or Code
One of nine broad job categories used on the EEO-1 Report. They are Officials & Managers, Professionals, Technicians, Sales Workers, Office & Clerical, Craft Workers, Operatives, Laborers, and Service Workers.

EEO-1 Report (See Employer Information Report (EEO-1)

Equal Pay Act of 1963
A federal law that bars employers from paying different wages to men and women who are performing equal work. Generally, the work of two employees is considered equal when both jobs require equal skill, effort, and responsibility and are performed under similar working conditions. EPA also applies to labor unions.

Establishment
A facility or unit that produces goods or services such as a factory, office, store, or mine. In most instances, the unit is a physically separate facility at a single location. In appropriate circumstances, OFCCP may consider as an establishment several facilities located at two or more sites when facilities are in the same labor market or recruiting area. The determination as to whether it is appropriate to group facilities as a single establishment will be made by OFCCP on a case-by-case basis.

Ethnic Group
A group identified on the basis of religion, color, or national origin.

Executive Orders 11246, 11375, and 12086
Regulations promulgated by the President that have the effect of law on those governmental matters with which they deal. These orders require contractors with contracts of $10,000 or more to provide equal employment opportunity on the basis of race, color, religion, sex, and national origin. These orders also require the preparation of a written affirmative action plan for contractors with $50,000 or more in contracts and 50 or more employees.

Goal Achievement
How well a contractor has progressed toward meeting employment or promotion targets set to correct under-utilization of protected class members.

Good Faith Efforts
Actions voluntarily developed by contractors to achieve compliance with equal employment opportunity and affirmative action clauses. The basic components of good faith efforts are: (1) outreach and recruitment measures to broaden candidate pools from which selection decisions are made to include minorities and women; and (2) systematic efforts to ensure that selections thereafter are made without regard to race, sex, or other prohibited factors. Results of these efforts are measured in terms of their effectiveness in assisting the contractor in meeting or making progress toward targets set to correct under-utilization.

Government Contract
Any agreement or modification thereof between any contracting agency and any person for the furnishing of supplies or services, or for the use of real or personal property, including lease arrangements. The term "services," as used here, includes, but is not limited to, the following: utility, construction, transportation, research, insurance, and fund depository, regardless of whether the Government is the purchaser or seller. The term "Government Contract" does not include (a) agreements in which the parties stand in the relationship of employer and employee and (b) Federally assisted construction contracts. See 41 CFR§§60-1.3, 250.2 and 741.2.

Hispanic
A person of Mexican, Puerto Rican, Cuban, Central or South American, or other Spanish culture or origin, regardless of race. This does not include persons of Portuguese descent or persons from Central or South America who are not of Spanish origin or culture.

Impact Ratio
Selection rate, for an employment opportunity, of a group of people in a protected class, divided by the selection rate of the group with the highest selection rate. For an adverse employment situation, the impact ratio is the rate of the group with the lowest rate divided by the rate of the group in question. Impact ratios are compared to the 80% Rule to determine adverse impact.

Individual with a Disability

Any person who:

a) has a physical or mental impairment which substantially limits one or more of such person's life activities;

b) has a record of such an impairment; or

c) is regarded as having such an impairment.

This definition does not include an individual currently engaging in the illegal use of drugs, when the contractor acts on the basis of such use. This definition does not include an individual who is an alcoholic whose current abuse of alcohol prevents such individual from performing the duties of the job in question or whose employment, by reason of such current alcohol abuse, would constitute a direct threat to property or safety of others.

The term "individual with a disability" is used interchangeably with "disabled individual".

Invitation to Self-Identify

An invitation by an employer extended to all employees who believe they are covered by Section 402 or 503 to identify themselves as having a disability, being a disabled veteran, a Vietnam era veteran, or other protected veteran for purposes of making reasonable accommodation and taking affirmative action. Applicants may no longer be asked to self-identify prior to an offer of employment being extended to them by the employer.

Job Area Acceptance Range (JAAR)

The JAAR is an analytical tool used to analyze the distribution of employees in a workforce by comparing the actual percentage of minorities/women in a job area to their percentage in the relevant larger segment of the contractor's workforce.

Job Categories

The nine designated categories of the EEO-1 report: officials and managers, professionals, technicians, sales workers, office and clerical, craft workers (skilled), operatives (semi-skilled), laborers (unskilled), and service workers.

Job Group
A division within the contractor's workforce for the purposes of analyzing the workforce for under-utilization. Job grouping is done to group job titles together based on similarity of job content, pay rates, and opportunities for advancement.

Labor Force
The total of all people in the civilian labor force and the armed forces.

Layoff
The process by which workers are removed from the active payroll to the inactive payroll during a reduction in force (RIF).

Life Activity
For purposes of Section 503 of the Rehabilitation Act and ADA, functions which are limited by a person's disability such as caring for oneself, performing manual tasks, walking, seeing, hearing, speaking, breathing, learning, and working.

Line of Progression
A series of related jobs in a promotional sequence generally starting with less difficult, lower paying jobs and progressing to more difficult, higher-paying jobs. Often, the lower jobs provide required training for movement to the higher-level jobs.

Make Whole Relief
Remedies for discrimination that restore the victim of discrimination to his or her rightful place, i.e., the position, both economically and in terms of employment status that he/she would have occupied had the discrimination never taken place. Common elements of make whole relief include an award of the position the individual was wrongfully denied, back pay with interest, and retroactive seniority.

Mandatory Job Listing (MJL)
The provision of the affirmative action clause at 41 CFR§250.4 that requires covered employers to list suitable job openings with the local office of the State Employment Service.

Minorities
Men and women of those minority groups for whom EEO-1 reporting is required; that is, black, Hispanic, Asian or Pacific Islander, American Indian or Alaskan Native. The term may refer to these groups in the aggregate or to an individual group.

National Origin
The country, including those that no longer exist, of one's birth or of one's ancestors' birth. "National origin" and "ethnicity" often are used interchangeably, although "ethnic group" can refer to religion or color, as well as country of one's ancestry.

Newly Separated Veteran
Any veteran who served on active duty in the U.S. military, ground, naval or air service during the one-year period beginning on the date of such veteran's discharge or release from active duty.

New Hire
A worker added to an establishment's payroll for first time.

Noncompliance
Failure to follow equal employment opportunity or affirmative action guidelines and the regulations applicable to them.

Notice of Violation (NOV)
A letter from OFCCP notifying the contractor that the agency has found violations of Executive Order 11246, Section 503 and/or 38 U.S.C.§4212 during a compliance evaluation, and the remedies that are required to resolve those violations.

Office of Federal Contract Compliance Programs (OFCCP)
Division of the Employment Standards Administration in the Department of Labor responsible for enforcing three statutes for federal contractors and subcontractors: Executive Order No. 11246, the Rehabilitation Act, and the Vietnam Era Veterans' Readjustment Assistance Act. OFCCP enforces the three laws through the use of compliance evaluations, complaint investigations, administrative procedures, and judicial procedures.

On-the-Job Training (OJT)
An employer sanctioned training program, usually at the employer's work site, conducted either under close supervision or with assistance and designed to teach and qualify an individual to perform a job or element(s) of a job.

Organizational Display
An organizational display is a detailed graphical or tabular chart, text, spreadsheet, or similar presentation of the contractor's organizational structure. It must identify each organizational unit in the establishment, and show the relationship of each organizational unit to the other organizational units in the establishment.

Organizational Profile
An organizational profile is a depiction of the staffing pattern within an establishment. It is one method contractors use to determine whether barriers to equal employment opportunity exist in their organizations. It provides an overview of the workforce at the establishment that may assist in identifying organizational units where women or minorities are under-represented or concentrated.

Organizational Unit
An organizational unit is any component that is part of the contractor's corporate structure. In a more traditional organization, it might be a department, division, section, branch, or group. In a less traditional organization, it might be a project team or job family.

Other Protected Veteran
A veteran who served on active duty in the U.S. military, ground, naval or air service during a war or in a campaign or expedition for which a campaign badge has been authorized.

Pattern or Practice Discrimination
Employer actions constituting a pattern of conduct resulting in discriminatory treatment toward the members of a class. Pattern or practice discrimination generally is demonstrated in large measures through statistical evidence and can be proven under either the disparate treatment or disparate impact model.

Physical & Mental Job Qualifications Requirement
Physical and mental standards that an employer requires a person performing or applying for a job to meet.

Placement Goals
Placement goals serve as objectives or targets reasonably attainable by applying good faith efforts to employment and promotion activities. Placement goals are used to measure progress toward achieving equal employment opportunity. Placement goals may not be rigid and inflexible quotas, which are forbidden.

Promotion
Any personnel action resulting in movement to a position affording higher pay and/or greater skill or responsibility, or the opportunity to attain such.

Protected Class
Groups of people protected from discrimination under government regulations and laws. The specific groups are defined as women, Blacks, Hispanics, Asians/Pacific Islanders or American Indians/Alaskan Natives, people over 40, the disabled as defined under Section 503 of the Rehabilitation Act and disabled veterans and Vietnam era veterans as defined under the Vietnam Era Veterans' Readjustment Assistance Act.

Qualified Disabled Veteran
A special disabled veteran who is capable of performing a particular job with or without a reasonable accommodation to his or her disability.

Qualified Disabled Person
A Qualified Disabled Person is an individual with a disability who is capable of performing a particular job, with or without reasonable accommodation.

Race
Race is a division of humankind with certain distinguishing characteristics in common which indicate distinctive origins.

Reasonable Accommodation
Used in connection with affirmative action for disabled persons: Changes in the job or workplace which enable the person with a disability to perform the job for which they are otherwise qualified. Such accommodations should be such that they do not create a business hardship and may involve such actions as adjusting the physical environment, equipment, schedules, or procedures. Used in connection with discrimination based on religion: Requirement that employer grant an employee time off for religious reasons. These accommodations may be adjustments to hours or days worked or other similar actions, which will make it possible for employees to fulfill their religious obligations.

Reasonable Recruitment Area
The area from which the contractor usually seeks or reasonably could seek workers for a particular job group.

Recall
The process or action by which workers are returned to active employment from layoff.

Recently Separated Veteran (See Newly Separated Veteran)

Recruiting Source
Any person, organization, or agency used to refer or provide workers for employment.

Red Circling
The practice of paying employees above the maximum of an established pay range. The rates of pay of such employees are "red circled".

Rehabilitation Act of 1973
Federal law requiring contractors and subcontractors with contracts in excess of $10,000 to take affirmative action to employ and advance in employment individuals with disabilities.

Rehire
To reengage a formerly employed worker after a complete break in employment status. Compare with "Recall."

Religion
Includes all aspects of religious observance and practice and religious beliefs.

Religious Accommodation
Requirement of a contractor to accommodate sincere religious observances and practices of an employee or prospective employee unless the contractor can demonstrate that it is unable to do so without undue hardship on the conduct of its business. See 41 CFR§60-50.3. Anything requiring more than a de minimis cost has been held by the Supreme Court to constitute "undue hardship" in this context.

Requisite Skills
Those basic skills needed to perform a job satisfactorily.

Selection Process
Any step, combination of steps, or procedure used as a basis for any employment decision, including but not limited to: informal or casual interviews; unscored application forms; paper and pencil tests; performance tests; training programs; probationary periods; and physical, education, and work experience requirements, as well as the decision making process used in determining whether or not to hire or promote.

Seniority
Length of employment as defined by the employer or applicable collective bargaining agreement. (Seniority may be both competitive and non-competitive and may be defined in terms of company seniority, facility seniority, departmental seniority, etc.) Employees may have different seniority for different purposes (e.g., job-bidding rights governed by department seniority and leave accrual governed by company seniority).

Sex Discrimination
Discriminatory or disparate treatment of persons based on their gender.

Show Cause Notice

A letter from OFCCP to the contractor ordering it to show why enforcement proceedings should not be instituted. A show cause notice follows OFCCP's issuance of a notice of violation and failure of conciliation. The show cause notice provides that the contractor must come into compliance within 30 days of OFCCP will recommend the institution of enforcement proceedings.

Special Disabled Veteran

(i) a veteran of the U.S. military, ground, naval or air service who is entitled to compensation (or who but for the receipt of military retirement pay would be entitled to compensation) under laws administered by the Department of Veterans' Affairs for a disability (A) rated at 30 percent or more, or (B) rated at 10 or 20 percent in the case of a veteran who has been determined under Section 38 U.S.C. 3106 to have a serious employment handicap or (ii) a person who was discharged or released from active duty because of a service-connected disability.

Standard Deviation

A statistical measure used to describe the probability that difference between similarly situated groups (such as in selection rates, wages, etc.) occurred by chance.

Subcontract

Any agreement or arrangement between a contractor and any person (in which the parties do not stand in the relationship of an employer and an employee):

(a) for the furnishing of supplies or services or for the use of real or personal property, including lease arrangements, which or in part, is necessary to the performance of any one or more Government contracts; or

(b) under which any portion of the contractor's obligation under one or Government contracts is performed, undertaken or assumed. See 41 CFR§60-1.3.

Subcontractor
Any person holding a subcontract, or for enforcement purposes, any person who has held a subcontract, subject to Executive Order 11246, Section 503 or 38 U.S.C.§4212. See definition of "Subcontract."

Substantially Limits
In the application of Section 503, this means to affect significantly an individual's ability to perform a major life activity, or to restrict significantly an individual as to the condition, manner, or duration under which such individual can perform a particular major life activity. The following factors should be considered when determining whether an individual is substantially limited in a major life activity: (a) The nature and severity of the impairment; (b) The duration or expected duration of the impairment; and (c) The permanent or long term impact, or the expected permanent or long term impact resulting from the impairment.

Systemic Discrimination
Employment policies or practices that serve to differentiate or to perpetuate a differentiation in terms or conditions of employment of applicants or employees because of their status as members of a particular group. Such policies or practices may or may not be fair and neutral on their face, and intent to discriminate may or may not be involved. Systemic discrimination, sometimes called class discrimination or a pattern or practice of discrimination, concerns a recurring practice or continuing policy rather than an isolated act of discrimination.

Termination
Separation of an employee from the active and inactive payroll.

Training
a) **Formal:** A structured program, often in a classroom setting, to develop an individual's skills and abilities. Some or all aspects of on-the-job training may fall into this category.

b) **Informal:** Experience-oriented training to increase an individual's skills and abilities. Typically, most aspects of on-the-job training fall into this category.

Transfer
Movement (usually lateral) from one position or function to another.

Underutilization
Having materially fewer minorities or women in a particular job group than reasonably would be expected based on their availability in the community.

Undue Hardship
In order for an employer to legally refuse to accommodate an applicant's or an employee's disability or religious beliefs, the employer must be able to show that such an accommodation would place a severe burden on the operation of the business.

Unlawful Employment Practice
Any policy or practice that has discriminatory intent or effect and cannot be shown to be essential to the successful performance of the job in question.

Validation
The study of an employer's test or selection standards which proves that they are significant predictors of successful job performance (i.e., those who score high turn out to be successful on a job and those who score low turn out to be unsuccessful). The study requires a large sample of applicants and must include representatives of groups - minorities and women, etc. - who may be suffering adversely from such standards.

Veterans Employment Opportunities Act
This statute extended the affirmative action and reporting responsibilities of Federal contractors and subcontractors, which previously protected veterans of the Vietnam era and special disabled veterans, to include any other U.S. veteran who served on active duty during a war or in a campaign or expedition for which a campaign badge was authorized. It also raised the reporting threshold from $10,000 to $25,000 and added the requirement to report the maximum and minimum number of persons employed on the VETS-100 report.

Vietnam Era Veteran
A person who (i) served on active duty in the U.S. military, ground, naval or air service for a period of more than 180 days, and who was discharged or released therefrom with other than a dishonorable discharge, if any part of such active duty was performed: (A) in the Republic of Vietnam between February 28, 1961, and May 7, 1975; or (B) between August 5, 1964, and May 7, 1975, in all other cases; or (ii) was discharged or released from active duty in the U.S. military, ground, naval or air service for a service-connected disability if any part of such active duty was performed: (A) in the Republic of Vietnam between February 28, 1961, and May 7, 1975; or (B) between August 5, 1964, and May 7, 1975, in any other location.

Vietnam Era Veterans' Readjustment Assistance Act of 1974
Federal law requiring federal contractors or subcontractors with contracts of $10,000 or more to take affirmative action to employ and advance in employment disabled veterans or those who served during the Vietnam era.

White
An individual, not of Hispanic origin, with origins in any of the original peoples of Europe, North Africa, or the Middle East.

Witnessed Counseling
The practice of conducting employee counseling sessions with more than one representative of management present (e.g. a manager and human resource representative; or a first line supervisor and second level manager).

Workforce Analysis
A listing of each job title as the title appears in applicable collective bargaining agreements or payroll records ranked from the lowest paid to the highest paid within each department including department or unit supervision. For each job title, the following information must be given: the total number of male and female employees; the total number of male and female employees who are Black (not Hispanic), Hispanic, American Indian/Alaskan Native, and Asian/Pacific Islander; and the wage rate or salary range.

Wrongful Discharge

Generally, unlawful employment termination. The phrase "wrongful discharge" is frequently used to refer to exceptions created by the courts in some states to the employment-at-will doctrine. Courts in such states differ in the circumstances in which they will allow wrongful discharge suits challenging a termination. State law on this issue is not of direct concern to OFCCP. Executive Order 11246, Section 503 or 38 U.S.C.§4212 and implementing regulations prohibit termination based on a prohibited factor.

APPENDIX B

POSITIVE OUTREACH AND RECRUITMENT

This appendix contains a directory of resources that companies may find useful in their positive outreach and recruitment efforts. It is not intended to be a comprehensive listing of all possible sources. Rather, it is a starting place to help begin the design and implementation of an affirmative action program.

The authority and usefulness of the resources and organizations listed cannot be guaranteed. These organizations are listed for informational purposes only. In particular, exercise caution when advertising in unfamiliar in media. Verify reasonable value for budget dollars expended. Use of any of the organizations listed in this appendix will not necessarily guarantee a successful outcome on an OFCCP compliance evaluation.

This resource or directory is organized into three broad categories:

1. Colleges and Universities that have a large proportion of minority students.

2. National associations and organizations that represent the interests of minorities, women, the disabled, and veterans.

3. *Examples* of local agencies, social service agencies or human service agencies that you may find in your community. The OFCCP refers to them as "linkage" agencies.

Under each category, there are suggested ways in which to build relationships with these sources. The nature and extent of the relationship will depend on the size and nature of the organization, the industry it is in, the geographic location, and recruitment and hiring activity including types of positions.

In using this directory, keep in mind the following:

- The resources listed here are <u>only suggestions</u>. This directory was complied to illustrate examples. Effective outreach efforts must support each company's needs and requirements. Additional research is necessary to craft a program that will be effective and appropriate for each company.

- There will be other, more targeted resources in local communities. They can be identified by consulting references in local libraries as well as local telephone directories and the Internet. These sources can also provide the address and phone number of some of those suggested resources, such as the Urban League, NAACP, local office of Veterans Affairs, or Goodwill Industries.

- Human rights agencies that investigate employment discrimination often can provide information on local community events and outreach sources. More information about these agencies is available by contacting the International Association of Official Human Rights Agencies at (202) 624-5410.

- The local offices of the OFCCP will often have knowledge of local organizations or resources to help increase workforce diversity. Contact information for the OFCCP is available through the Department of Labor's web site at:
  http://www.dol.gov/dol/esa/public/contacts/ofccp/ofcpkeyp. htm

- The nature of the relationship established with these resources should align with an individual company's need. Recruiting entry-level skills will require a focus on local agencies rather than professional associations or colleges. Nevertheless, a cross section of resources from the categories listed should be considered. For example, select some schools, some professional organizations, and some local agencies. More detailed discussions of the types of activities that can be pursued with each can be found later in this directory.

- In making selections of agencies, keep in mind the types of jobs and skill sets needed. For example, if hiring individuals with information technology backgrounds, <u>consider</u> an organization such as Women in Technology International.

- The number of resources with which relationships are established should align with the company size and recruitment activity. The larger the company, the greater the number of relationships.

- Vary the resources used from year to year. If the resources chosen are not effective in helping meet placement rate goals, try others in subsequent years.

- Keep in mind that if the OFCCP determines that Good Faith Efforts and Action-Oriented Programs are not sufficient, they will require a company to establish relationships with organizations that they choose.

Colleges & Universities

Included in this section is a listing of colleges and universities that traditionally enroll a large proportion of minority students. In choosing schools with which to establish relationships, choose those offering courses of study that align with the company's needs. In other words, don't establish a relationship with a Liberal Arts college if hiring students with engineering degrees only. Also, research community colleges and vocational or trade schools in your community, if appropriate, for recruiting and hiring needs.

The following are some—<u>suggested</u> activities in which a contractor can engage:

- If a significant number of students are hired right out of college, participate in job fairs sponsored by the school or invite them to company sponsored events.
- Consider establishing an internship program and inviting students from select schools to participate.
- Participate in campus recruiting events.
- Meet with placement officers at the schools and advise them of the types of positions for which the company recruits. Ask them to refer students.
- Post available job positions on their web sites or establish links between the school's web site and the company web site.
- Arrange to have company representatives speak to student groups.
- If only occasional college hires are made, consider sending the schools a letter similar to the one on the following page that encourages the placement office to refer students to your web site.

SAMPLE INTRODUCTORY LETTER TO COLLEGES & UNIVERSITIES

Date

Name
Address

Dear _____,

[Company] is dedicated to complying with its obligations of Equal Employment Opportunity and Affirmative Action in all employment practices. We have an on-going commitment to hire and develop the best people, based on job-related qualifications. Accordingly, all applicants will be treated fairly. Our recruiting and hiring procedures are free of unlawful discrimination based on race, color, sex, age, disability status, religion, national origin, marital status, sexual orientation, ancestry, political belief or activity, or U. S. veteran status.

As part of our Affirmative Action Program, we are committed to encouraging qualified applicants to seek employment with us. We encourage you to refer your students to our web site so they can familiarize themselves with our company and explore potential career opportunities. A list of our open positions, along with information about the company, can be found on our web site at **www.companyname.com**.

We appreciate your support in referring candidates to our company. Please call me should you have any questions. My number is _____.

Sincerely,

Colleges & Universities with a High Number of Minority Students (by state)

African-American Students

Alabama Agricultural & Mechanical University
P.O. Box 908
Normal, AL 35762
Placement Office: 205-851-5410
Fax: (205) 851-5244
www.aamu.edu

Alabama State University
915 S. Jackson Street
Montgomery, AL 36104
Placement Office: 334-229-4140
www.alasu.edu

Tuskegee University
Tuskegee, AL 36088
Placement Office: (334) 727-8146
Fax: (334) 727-8258
www.tusk.edu

**University of Arkansas
at Pine Bluff**
1200 University Drive
Pine Bluff, AR 71601
Placement Office: (870) 575-8000
www.uapb.edu

California State University – Fresno
5150 N. Maple Drive
Fresno, CA 93740
Placement Office: (559) 278-2381
Fax: (559) 278-6483
www.csufresno.edu

**California State University –
Los Angeles**
5151 State University
Los Angeles, CA 90032
(323) 343-3000
Placement Office: (323) 343-3649
www.calstatela.edu

California State University – Northridge
18111 Nordhoff Street
Northridge, CA 91330
Placement Office: (818) 677-2878
Fax: (818) 677-4593
www.csun.edu

Florida Agricultural & Mechanical University
Career Center
Student Union Plaza, Suite 100
Tallahassee, FL 32307
(850) 599-8514
Placement Office: (850) 599-3700
Fax: (850) 599-3353
www.famu.edu

Albany State University
504 College Drive
Albany, GA 31705
(229) 430-4600
Placement Office: (229) 430-4646
http://asweb.asurams.edu

Clark Atlanta University
223 S. James T. Brawley Dr. SW
Atlanta, GA 30314
(404) 880-8000
www.cau.edu

Morehouse College
830 Westview Drive, SW
Atlanta, GA 30314
(404) 681-2800
Placement Office: (404) 215-2862
www.morehouse.edu

Savannah State University
3219 College Street/P.O. Box 20376
Savannah, GA 31404
(912) 356-2181
Placement Office: (912) 356-2285
Fax: (912) 691-5556
www.savstate.edu

Chicago State University
9501 South King Drive
Chicago, IL 60628
(773) 995-2000
Placement Office: (773) 995-2327
Fax: (773) 995-2329
www.csu.edu

Grambling State University
GSU Box 4264
Grambling, LA 71245
Placement Office: (318) 274-3828
Fax: (318) 274-3357
(800) 569-4714
www.gramu.edu

**Southern Univ. Agricultural &
Mechanical College**
P.O. Box 10980
Baton Rouge, LA 70813
(225) 771-4500
Placement Office: (225) 771-2200
Fax: (225) 771-3272
www.subr.edu

Xavier University of Louisiana
1 Drexel Avenue
New Orleans, LA 70125
(504) 486-7411
Placement Office: (504) 483-7364
www.xula.edu

Coppin State College – Career
Development
2500 West North Avenue
Baltimore, MD 21216
(410) 951-3000
(800) 635-3674
Placement Office: (410) 383-5900
www.coppin.edu

Morgan State University
1700 Cold Spring Lane
Baltimore, MD 21251
(443) 885-3333
www.morgan.edu

Alcorn State University
PO Box 359/1000 ASU Drive
Lorman, MS 39096
Placement Office: (601) 877-6100
(601) 877-6111
Fax: (601) 877-2875
www.alcorn.edu

Jackson State University
1400 John R. Lynch
Jackson, MS 39217
(601) 979-2477
Fax: (601) 979-2816
www.jsums.edu

**NC Agricultural & Technical State
University**
1601 East Market Street
Greensboro, NC 27411
(336) 334-7500
Placement Office: (336) 334-7755
Fax: (336) 334-7018
www.ncat.edu

North Carolina Central University
1801 Fayetteville Street
Durham, NC 27707
(919) 530-6100
Placement Office: (919) 560-6337
www.nccu.edu/careerservices

**Medger Evers College – City University of
NY**
1150 Carroll Street
Brooklyn, NY 11225
Career Development: (718) 270-6055
www.mec.cuny.edu

Central State University
P.O. Box 1004
Wilberforce, OH 45384
Placement Office: (937) 376-6383
(937) 376-6011
www.centralstate.edu

South Carolina State University
300 College Street, NE/Box 7068
Orangeburg, SC 29117
(803) 536-7000
Placement Office: (803) 536-7033
Fax: (803) 533-3622
www.scsu.edu

Tennessee State University
3500 John Merritt Boulevard
Nashville, TN 37209
(615) 320-3432
Placement Office: (615) 963-5981
Fax: (615) 963-7534
www.tnstate.edu

Prairie View Agricultural & Mechanical University
Career Planning & Placement
PO Box 519
Prairie View, TX 77446
(936) 857-3311
Placement Office: (936) 857-2055
www.pvamu.edu

Texas Southern University
3100 Cleburne
EO Building, Room 207
Houston, TX 77004
(713) 313-7011
Placement Office: (713) 313-7346
www.tsu.edu

Hampton University
Career Counseling
Wigwam Building 114
Hampton, VA 23668
(757) 727-5331
Placement Office: (757) 727-5000
www.hamptonu.edu

Norfolk State University
Career Services
700 Park Avenue
Norfolk, VA 23504
(757) 683-8600
Placement Office: (757) 823-8462
Fax: (757) 823-2075
www.nsu.edu

Virginia State University
Career Planning and Placement
PO Box 9410
Petersburg, VA 23806
(804) 524-5000
Placement Office: (804) 524-5211
Fax: (804) 524-5212
www.vsu.edu

Howard University – Career Center
525 Bryant Street NW
Washington, DC 20059
(202) 806-7513
www.howard.edu

University of the District of Columbia
4200 Cohn Avenue NW
Washington, DC 20008
(202) 274-5000
Placement Office: (202) 274-5111
www.udc.edu

Hispanic-American Students

**University of California
– Berkeley**
2111 Bancroft Way
Berkeley, CA 94720
Placement Office: (510) 642-1716
Fax: (510) 643-6120
www.berkeley.edu

**University of California –
Los Angeles**
Box 951573
Los Angeles, CA 90059
Placement Office: (310) 206-1941
http://career.ucla.edu

University of Southern Colorado
2200 Bonforte Boulevard
Pueblo, CO 81001
(719) 549-2461
Placement Office: (719) 549-2512
www.uscolo.edu

Barry University
11300 NE Second Avenue
Miami Shores, FL 33161
(305) 899-3000 (800) 756-6000
Placement Office: (305) 899-3950
Fax: (305) 899-3487
www.barry.edu

Florida International University
11200 SW 8th Street
Miami, FL 33199
(305) 348-2000
Placement Office: (305) 348-2423
www.fiu.edu

St. Thomas University
16400 NW 32 Avenue
Miami, FL 33054
(305) 625-6000
Placement Office: (305) 828-6688/6690
www.stu.edu

University of Miami
P.O. Box 249175
Coral Gables, FL 33124
(305) 284-2211
Placement Office: (305) 284-5451
www.miami.edu

Kean University of New Jersey
1000 Morris Avenue
Union, NJ 07083
(908) 737-5326
Placement Office: (908) 737-5830
www.kean.edu

Eastern New Mexico University
1200 W. University
Portales, NM 88130
(505) 562-1011
Placement Office: (505) 562-2211
www.enmu.edu

New Mexico Highlands University
Las Vegas, NM 87701
(505) 454-3439
Placement Office: (505) 454-3470
www.nmhu.edu

New Mexico State University
Las Cruces, NM 88003
(505) 646-0111
Placement Office: (505) 646-1631
www.nmsu.edu

University of New Mexico
Albuquerque, NM 87131
(505) 277-0111
Placement Office: (505) 277-2531
Fax: (505) 277-9285
www.unm.edu

Baruch College of the City University of NY
1 Bernard Baruch Way
New York, NY 10010
(646) 312-1000
Placement Office: (646) 312-4683
Fax: (646) 312-4670
www.baruch.cuny.edu

105

**City College of the City
University of NY**
Convent Avenue @ 138 Street
New York, NY 10031
(212) 650-7000
Placement Office: (212) 650-5326
www.ccny.cuny.edu

Hunter College of the City University
695 Park Avenue
New York, NY 10021
(212) 772-4000
Placement Office: (212) 772-4850
Fax: (212) 772-5438
www.hunter.cuny.edu

Mercy College
555 Broadway
Dobbs Ferry, NY 10522
(800)MERCY-NY
Placement Office: (914) 674-7203
www.mercynet.edu

Our Lady of the Lake Univ. of San Antonio
411 SW 24 Street
San Antonio, TX 78207
Placement Office: (210) 434-6711 ext 249
www.ollusa.edu

St. Edwards University
3001 S. Congress Avenue
Austin, TX 78704
(512) 448-8400
Placement Office: (512) 448-8530
www.stedwards.edu

**St. Mary's University of
San Antonio**
One Camino Santa Maria
San Antonio, TX 78228
Placement Office: (210) 4363102
Fax: (210) 431-2231
www.stmarytx.edu

**Texas A & M University –
Corpus Christi**
6300 Ocean Drive
Corpus Christi, TX 78413
Placement Office: (361) 825-2629
Fax: (361) 825-5729
www.tamucc.edu

Texas A & M University
College Station, TX 77843
(979) 845-3211
Placement Office: (979) 845-5139
Fax: (979) 845-2979
www.tamu.edu

University of Houston – Downtown
One Main Street
Houston, TX 77002
(713) 221-8000
Placement Office: (713) 743-221-8980
Fax: (713) 221-8076
www.dt.uh.edu

University of Texas – El Paso
500 W. University Drive
El Paso, TX 79968
(915) 747-5000
Placement Office: (915) 747-5640
Fax: (915) 747-5730
www.utep.edu

University of Texas – Pan American
1201 W. University Drive
Edinburgh, TX 78539
(956) 381-2011
Placement Office: (956) 381-2243
Fax: (956) 381-2996
www.panam.edu

University of Texas – San Antonio
6900 N. Loop 1604 W
San Antonio, TX 78249
(210) 458-4011
Placement Office: (210) 458-4589
www.utsa.edu

Asian-American Students

University of Southern California
University Park Campus
Los Angeles, CA 90089
(213) 740-2311
Placement Office: (213) 740-9111
www.usc.edu

Yale University
55 Whitney Avenue/P.O. Box 280303
New Haven, CT 06520
Placement Office: (203) 432-0803
Fax: (203) 432-7184
www.yale.edu

University of Hawaii-Manoa
2444 Dole Street
Honolulu, HI 96822
(808) 956-8111
Placement Office: (808) 956-8136
www.hawaii.edu

University of Chicago
1212 East 59 Street
Chicago, IL 60637
(773) 702-1234
Placement Office: (773) 702-7040
www.uchicago.cdu

University of Illinois at Chicago
1200 West Harrison
Chicago, IL 60607
(312) 996-7000
Placement Office: :(312) 996-2300
Fax: (312) 413-0383
www.uic.edu

University of Pennsylvania
3451 Walnut Street
Philadelphia, PA 19104
(215) 898-5000
Placement Office: (215) 898-3208
www.upenn.edu

University of Washington
Box 352810
Seattle, WA 98195
(206) 543-2100
Placement Office: (206) 543-0535
www.washington.edu

Native American Students

University of Alaska-Anchorage
3211 Providence Drive
Anchorage, AK 99508
(907) 786-1800
Placement Office: (907) 786-4513
www.uaa.alaska.edu

University of Alaska-Fairbanks
P.O. Box 757520
Fairbanks, AK 99775
Placement Office: (907) 474-6644
Fax: (907) 474-6176
www.uaf.edu

Northern Arizona University
S. San Francisco Street
Flagstaff, AZ 86011
(928) 523-9011
(888) MORE NAU
Placement Office: (928) 523-3357
www.nau.edu

Fort Lewis College Career Services
1000 Rim Drive
Durango, CO 81301
(970) 247-7010
Placement Office: (970) 247-7562
Fax: (970) 247-7653
www.fortlewis.edu

University of Hawaii at Hilo
200 West Kawili Street
Hilo, HI 96720
(800) 897-4456
Placement Office: (808) 544-0230
www.uhh.hawaii.edu

Montana State University – Northern
P.O. Box 7751
Havre, MT 59501
(406) 265-3700
(800) 662-6132
Placement Office: (406) 265-3708
www.nmclites.edu

University of North Carolina – Pembroke
P.O. Box 1510
Pembroke, NC 28372
(910) 521-6000
(800) 949-8627
Placement Office: (910) 521-6270

University of Mary
7500 University Drive
Bismarck, ND 58504
(800) 408-6279
Placement Office: (701) 255-7500
ext 414
www.umary.edu

East Central University
Ada, OK 74820
(580) 322-8000
Placement Office: (580) 310-5260
Fax: (580) 310-5484
www.ecok.edu

Northeastern State University
607 North Grand Avenue
Tahlequah, OK 74464
(800) 722-9614
Placement Office: (918) 456-5511
ext 3111
Fax: (918) 458-2114
www.nsuok.edu

Southeastern Oklahoma State University
Durant, OK 74701
(580) 745-2270
(800) 435-1327
Placement Office: (580) 924-0121
Fax: (580) 745-7486
www.sosu.edu

University of Oklahoma
900 Asp Avenue OMU#323
Norman, OK 73019
Placement Office: (405) 325-3402
Fax: (405) 325-3402
www.ou.edu

University of Science and Art of Oklahoma
1727 West Alabama
Chickasha, OK 73018
(405)-224-3140
(800) 933-8726
Placement Office: (405) 224-3131
www.usao.edu

Heritage College
Toppenish, WA
Placement Office: (509) 865-2244
www.heritage.edu
Fax: (910) 521-6166
www.uncp.edu

Minority & Women Organizations

Included in this section is a listing of organizations that represent the interests of minorities and women. The majority of those listed are professional societies. Many of these organizations have local chapters. Check the local library (e.g., the Encyclopedia for Associations), phone book, the Internet, and other resources for the most up-to-date addresses and contact information and for information on local chapters. The information presented in the listing is a starting point for research. The following are some suggestions for establishing relationships with these organizations.

- Post jobs on their web sites or consider a link between their web site and the company's web site.
- Many of these organizations have student chapters at local colleges and universities. Contact these student chapters and arrange for a company representative to speak at their meetings. Invite the students for a tour and meeting with line managers. (See suggestions under Colleges and Universities.)
- If there are local chapters at the professional level, arrange to have company speakers at their meetings.
- Sponsor a meeting for a local chapter.
- Notify local chapters of position openings.
- If company representatives are active with local chapters, have them announce job openings or otherwise promote the organization. Consider accompanying the employee to a local meeting as a guest.
- Participate in career fairs or conferences.

Organizations for Minorities & Women

General

Chemical Industries for Minorities in Engineering (CHIME)
American Institute for Chemical Engineers
3 Park Avenue
New York, NY 10016
(800) 242-4363
www.aiche.org/careers/workplac.htm

Diversity/Careers in Engineering and Information Technology
197 Mountain Ave.
P.O. Box 557
Springfield, NJ 07081-0557
(973) 912-8550
www.diversitycareers.com

The Diversity Career Center
(503) 221-7779 OR
(603) 971-0771 CA
www.diversitysearch.com

Diversity Employment – Multicultural employment resource & resume database
Innovative Human Resources Solutions
801 W. El Camino Real
Mountain View, CA 94040-2511
Fax (408) 273-6467
www.diversityemployment.com

HireDiversity.com – Minority Professionals
(800) 810-7521
www.hirediversity.com

IMDiversity.com – Minority & Women
909 Poydras St. 36th Floor
New Orleans, LA 70112
(504) 523-0754
www.IMDiversity.com

Inroads – Internship programs for minority high school and college students
10 South Broadway, Suite 700
St. Louis, MO 63102
(312) 241-7488
www.inroads.org

Minority Career Network
P.O. Box 1131
Sugarland, TX 77487-1131
(281) 499-3481
www.minoritycareernet.com

Minorities in Agriculture, Natural Resources & Related Sciences (MANRRS)
P.O. Box 381017
6750 Poplar Avenue, Suite 718
Memphis, TN 38138
(908) 757-9700
www.manns.org

National Association of Minority Engineering Program Administrators (NAMEPA)
1133 West Morse Boulevard,
Suite 201
Winter Park, FL 32789
(407) 647-8839
www.namepa.org

National Action Council for Minorities in Engineering (NACME)
The Empire State Building
350 5th Ave., Suite 2212
New York, NY 10118
(212) 279-2626
www.nacme.org

National Association for Equal Opportunity in Higher Education (NAFEO)
8701 Georgia Ave., Suite 200
Silver Springs, MD 20910
(301) 650-2440
www.nafeo.org (under construction)

National Association of Minority Architects
413 Van Buren Street, NW
Washington, DC 20012
www.noma.net

National Coalition of 100 Black Women, Inc. (NCBW)
38 West 32nd Street, Suite 1610
New York, NY 10001-3816
(212) 947-2196
www.ncbw.org

National Consortium for Graduate Degrees for Minorities in Engineering and Science, Inc. (GEM)
The GEM Consortium Central Office
P.O. Box 537
Notre Dame, IN 46556
(574) 631-7771
http://was.nd.edu/gem/gemwebapp/
gem_00_000.htm

National Technical Association, Inc. (NTA)
NTA National Headquarters
6919 North 19th St.
Philadelphia, PA 19126-1506
(215) 549-5743
P.O. Box 710567
Houston, TX 77271
(877) 854-8041
www.ntaonline.org

Welfare Rights Organization
www.afrikana.com

Organizations for African-Americans

Additional Organizations –
www.eblackstudies.org/organizations.html
ABC Association of Black Cardiologists
6849-B2 Peachtree Dunwoody Road, NE
Atlanta, GA 30328
(301) 474-NABA
www.abcardio.org

African Scientific Institute
527 32nd Street
Oakland, CA 94609
(510) 653-7027

**The Association of Negro Business and
Professional Women's Clubs**
Washington, DC
(202) 483-4206
www.nanbpwc.org

Black Collegian
(504) 523-0154
www.black-collegian.com

Black Data Processing Association
9315 Largo Drive West, Suite 260
Largo, MD 20774
(800) 727-BDPA
www.bdpa.org

Black Human Resource Network (BHRN)
8855 Annapolis Road, Suite 301
Lanham, MD 20706
(301) 459-6200
www.bhrn.org

Black Voices
Tribune Tower
435 North Michigan Avenue,
Suite LL2
Chicago, IL 60611
(312) 222-4326
www.blackvoices.com

Black Women in Publishing (BWIP)
www.bwip.org

**African-American Women Business
Owners Association (AAWBOA)**
3363 Alden Place, NE
Washington, DC 20019
(202) 399-3645
http://www.blackpgs.com/aawboa. html

CORE Congress of Racial Equality
817 Broadway, 3rd Floor
New York, NY 10003
(212) 598-4000
www.core-online.org

**National Association for the Advancement
of Colored People – NAACP**
4805 Mount Hope Drive
Baltimore, MD 21215
(877)NAACP-98
(410) 521-4939
www.naacp.org

**National Association for Black Veterans
(NABV)**
(800) 842-4597
www.nabrets.com

**National Association of Black Accountants
(NABA)**
7249-A Hanover Parkway
Greenbelt, MD 20770
(301) 474-NABA
www.nabainc.org

National Black MBA Association
180 North Michigan Avenue,
Suite 1400
Chicago, IL 60601

(312) 236-2622
www.nbmbaa.org

National Black Nurses Association (NBNA)
8630 Fenton Street, Suite 330
Silver Spring, MD 20910
(301) 589-3200
www.nbna.org

**National Council of Black Engineers &
Scientists**
1525 Aviation Blvd., Suite C424
Redondo Beach, CA 90278
(213) 896-9779
www.ncbes.org

National Council of Negro Women
633 Pennsylvania Avenue
Washington DC, 20004
www.ncnw.org

**National Organization for Professional
Advancement of Black Chemists and
Chemical Engineers (NOBCCHE)**
Howard University,
525 College Ave.,
P.O. Box 5, NW
Washington, D.C. 20059

(202) 667-1699
www.nobcche.org

**National Society of Black Engineers
(NSBE)**
1454 Duke St.
Alexandria, VA 22314
(703) 549-2207
www.nsbe.org

National Society of Black Physicists (NSBP)
6704G Lee Highway
Arlington, VA 22205
(703) 536-4207
www.nsbp.org

National Urban League
120 Wall Street
New York, NY 10005
(888) 491-8833
(212) 558-5300
www.nul.org

United Negro College Fund
8260 Willow Oaks Corporate Drive
Fairfax, VA 22031
(703) 205-3400
(800) 331-2244
www.uncf.org

Organizations for Asian-Americans

Asian American Architects and Engineers
8320 Lincoln Boulevard, Suite 308
Los Angeles, CA 90045
(213) 896-9270
(213) 896-9271 fax
www.aaaesc.com

Asian American Journalists Association
1182 Market Street, Suite 320
San Francisco, CA 94102
(415) 346-2051
(415) 346-6343 fax
www.aaja.org

Asian Chamber of Commerce
1219 East Glendale Ave, Suite 25
Phoenix, AZ 85020
(602) 222-2009
(602) 870-7562 fax

Asian Pacific Americans Network
231 East Third Street, Suite G104
Los Angeles, CA 90013
www.apanet.org

Asian Pacific Environmental Network
310 8th Street, Suite 309
Oakland, CA 94607
Ph: 510-834-8920
Fax: 510-834-8926
www.apen4ej.org

Filipino American Society of Architects and Engineers
703 Market Street, Suite 711
San Francisco, CA 94103
(415) 957-1189
www.fasae.org

National Association of Asian American Professionals
(See website for state by state chapters)
www.naaap.org

National Association of Professional Asian American Women
18627 Carriage Walk Circle
Gaithersburg, MD 20879
(301) 869-8288
www.napaw.com

Organization of Chinese Americans
1001 Connecticut Avenue NW,
Suite 600
Washington, DC 20036
(202) 223-5500
(202) 296-0540 fax
www.ocanatl.org

Organizations for Hispanic-Americans

American Association of Hispanic CPA's
19726 East Colina Road, Suite 270
Rowland Heights, CA 91748
(626) 965-0643

**Association of Hispanic Advertising
Agencies**
8201 Greensboro Dr., Suite 300
McLean, VA 22102
(703) 610-9014
(703) 610-9005 fax
www.ahaa.org

**Association of Latino Professionals in
Finance and Accounting**
510 West Sixth Street, Suite 400
Los Angeles, CA 90014
(213) 243-0004
(213) 243-0006 fax
www.alfa.org

**Center for Advancement of Hispanics in
Science & Engineering Education
(CAHSEE)**
1444 Eye Street NW, Suite 800
Washington, DC 20005
(202) 422-7651
www.cahsee.org

Hispanic & Bilingual Professionals
20 North Clark Street, Suite 2900
Chicago, IL 60602
(312) 279-2000
www.iHispano.com

**Hispanic Association of Colleges and
Universities (HACU)**
8415 Datapoint Drive, Suite 400
San Antonio, TX 78229
(210) 692-3805 (voice)
(210) 692-0823 (fax)
www.hacu.net

**Hispanic Association on Corporate
Responsibility**
1730 Rhode Island Avenue, NW, Suite 1008
Washington, DC 20036
(202) 835-9672

Hispanic Business News
425 Pine Avenue
Santa Barbara, CA 93117-3709
(805) 964-4554
www.HispanicBusiness.com

Hispanic Elected Local Officials
1301 Pennsylvania Avenue, NW
Washington, DC 20004
(202) 626-3169

Hispanic Engineers and Scientists
104 Naval Architecture Building
University of California
Berkeley, CA 94720
(510) 643-8416
www.berkeleyhes.org

**Hispanic Organization of Latin Actors
(HOLA)**
250 West 65th Street
New York, NY 10023
(212) 595-8286

**Hispanic Organization of Professionals &
Executives (HOPE)**
1700 17th Street NW, Suite 405-2009
Washington, DC 20009
(202) 234-2351

Hispanic Public Relations Association
735 Figueroa, Suite 818
Los Angeles, CA 90017
(213) 239-6555 ext. 204
www.hprala.org

National Association of Hispanic County Officials
440 First Street, NW, 8th Floor
Washington, DC 20001
(202) 942-4260

National Association of Hispanic Federal Executives (NAHEE)
P.O. Box 469
Herndon, VA 20172-0469
(703) 787-0291

National Association of Hispanic Journalists
1193 National Press Building
Washington, DC 20045
(202) 662-7145

National Association of Hispanic & Latino Studies
Morehead State University
211 Radar Hall
Morehead, KY
(606) 783-2650

National Association of Hispanic Nurses
1501 16th Street, NW
Washington, DC 20036
(202) 387-2477

National Association of Hispanic Public Administrators
PO Box 42171
Coral Gables, FL 33114-2171
(305) 828-8999

National Association of Hispanic Publications
652 National Press Building
Washington, DC 20045
(202) 662-7250

National Association of Latino Elected & Appointed Officials
5800 S. Eastern Avenue, #365
Los Angeles, CA 90040
(323) 720-4321

National Association of Puerto Rican/ Hispanic Social Workers, Inc.
PO Box 651
Brentwood, NY 11717
(516) 864-1536
www.naprhsw.com

National Coalition of Hispanic Health and Human Services Organizations
1501 16th Street, NW
Washington, DC 20036
(202) 797-4321

National Federation of Hispanic Owned Newspapers
853 Broadway, Suite 811
New York, NY 10003
(212) 420-0009

National Hispanic Academy of Media, Arts, and Sciences
4457 Oak Street
Pico Rivera, CA 30660
(310) 712-5739

National Hispanic Bar Association
PO Box 66105
Washington, DC 20035
(202) 293-1507

National Hispanic Corporate Council
8201 Greensboro Drive, Suite 300
McLean, VA 22102
(703) 610-9016

National Hispanic Dental Association
188 W. Randolph Street, Suite 1811
Chicago, IL 60601
(312) 577-4013

National Hispanic Environmental Council
106 North Fayette Street
Alexandria, VA 22314
(703) 922-2439
(703) 922-3761 fax
www.nheec.org

National Hispanic Media Coalition
5400 E. Olympic Blvd., Suite 250
Los Angeles, CA 90022-5142
(323) 722-4191

National Hispanic Medical Organization
1700 17th Street, NW, Suite 405-2009
Washington, DC 20009
(202) 265-4297

National Latino Peace Officers Association
133 South West Blvd. #B
Rohnert Park, CA 94928
(877) 657-6200

National Society of Hispanic MBAs
1303 Walnut Hill Lane, Suite 300
Irving, TX 75038
(877) 467-4622
(214) 596-9325
www.nshmba.org

Saludos Hispanic
(800) 371-4456
www.saludos.com

Society for the Advancement of Chicanos & Native Americans in Science (SACNAS)
P.O. Box 8526
Santa Cruz, CA 95061-8526
(831) 459-0170
http://www.sacnas.org

Society of Hispanic Professional Engineers (SHPE)
5400 East Olympic Boulevard,
Suite 210
Los Angeles, CA 90022
(323) 725-3970
(323) 725-0316 fax
www.shpe.org

Society of Mexican American Engineers and Scientists (MAES)
13337 South Street, Suite 349
Cerritos, CA 90703
(714) 560-7732
www.maes-natl.org

Organizations for Native-Americans

American Indian Higher Education Consortium
121 Oronoco St.
Alexandria, VA 22314
(703) 838-0400
(703) 838-0388 fax
http://www.aihec.org

American Indian Science & Engineering Society
(AISES)
P.O. Box 9828
Albuquerque, NM 87119-9828
(505) 765-1052
(505) 765-5608 fax
http://www.aises.org

Bureau of Indian Affairs
(202) 208-3710
www.doi.gov/bureau-indian-affairs.html

First Nations Development Institute
The Stores Building
11917 Main St.
Fredericksburg, VA 22408
(540) 371-5615
http://www.firstnations.org

INMED Indians Into Medicine
501 North Columbus Road
Grand Forks, ND 58203
(701) 777-3037

National Congress of American Indians
1301 Connecticut Ave., NW,
Suite 200
Washington, D.C. 20036
(202) 466-7767
(202) 466-7797
http://www.ncai.org

National Tribal Environmental Council
2501 Rio Grande Blvd. NW, Suite A
Albuquerque, NM 87104
(505) 242-2175
http://www2.ntec.org

Native American Environmental Protection Coalition
42143 Avenida Alvarado, Unit 2A
Temecula, CA 92590
(877) 739-9234
(909) 296-5595

Native American Fish & Wildlife Society
750 Burbank St.
Broomfield, CO 80020
(303) 466-1725
www.nafws.org

Native American Rights Fund
1506 Broadway
Boulder, CO 80302
(303) 447-8760
(303) 443-7776
http://www.narf.org

Native American Water Association
1662 Highway 395, Suite 212
Minden, NV 89423
(702) 782-6636
www.nawainc.org

Tribal Employment Newsletter
25 Nob Hill Road
Limerick, ME 04048
(207) 793-9333
www.nativejobs.com

United Indians of all Tribes Foundations (UIATF)
Discovery Park
P.O. Box 99100
Seattle, WA 98199
(206) 285-4425
www.unitedindians.com

Organizations for Women

American Association of University Women (AAUW)
1111 Sixteenth Street NW
Washington DC 20036
(800) 326-AAUW
www.aauw.org

American Business Women's Association (ABWA)
9100 Ward Parkway
P.O. Box 8728
Kansas City, MO 64114-0728
(800) 228-0007
www.abwa.org

American Society of Women Accountants (ASWA)
8405 Greensboro Drive, Suite 800
McLean, VA 22102
(800) 326-2163
(703) 506-3265
www.aswa.org

Association for Women in Mathematics (AWM)
4114 Computer & Sciences Building
University of Maryland
College Park, MD 20742-2461
(301) 405-7892
www.awm-math.org

Association for Women in Science
1200 New York Avenue NW,
Suite 650
Washington, DC 20005
(202) 326-8940
www.awis.org

The Association of Negro Business and Professional Women's Clubs
1806 New Hampshire Avenue, NW
Washington, DC 20009
(202) 483-4206
www.nanbpwc.org

Black Women in Publishing (BWIP)
www.bwip.org
Career Women
805 SW Broadway, Suite 2250
Portland, OR 97205
(503) 221-7779
www.careerwoman.com

Federation of Organizations for Professional Women
P.O. Box 6234
Falls Church, VA 22040
(202) 328-1415
www.fopw.org

Financial Women's Association
215 Park Avenue South, Suite 1713
New York, NY 10003
(212) 533-2141
(212) 982-3008
www.fwa.org

Women in Aerospace (WIA)
P.O. Box 16721
Alexandria, VA 22302
(202) 547-9451
www.womeninaerospace.org

National Association of Female Executives
P.O. Box 469031
Escondido, CA 92046-9925
(800) 634-NAFE
www.nafe.com

National Council of Negro Women
633 Pennsylvania Avenue
Washington DC, 20004
www.ncnw.org

National Organization for Women (NOW)
www.now.org

Society for Women Engineers
230 East Ohio Street, Suite 400
Chicago, IL 60611-3265
(312) 596-5223
www.swe.org

Women in Advertising & Marketing
4200 Wisconsin Avenue NW,
Suite 106-238
Washington DC, 20016
(301) 369-7400
www.wamdc.org

Women Employed (WE)
111 North Wabash 13th Floor
Chicago IL 60602
(312) 782-3902
www.womenemployed.org

Women's Equity Action League
WEEA – Equity Resource Center
55 Chapel Street
Newton, MA 02458-1060
(800) 255-3088
www.edc.org/womensequity

Women in Engineering Program Advocates Network
1284 CIVL Building, Room G293
West Lafayette, IN 47907-1284
Phone (765) 494-5387
Fax (765) 494-9152
www.wepan.org

Women in Technology International
6345 Balboa Boulevard, Suite 257
Encino, CA 91316
(800) 334-WITI
www.witi.org

Organizations for Individuals with Disabilities

American Association of the Deaf-Blind
814 Thayer Avenue, Suite 302
Silver Spring, MD 20910
(301) 588-6545

American Disabilities Association(tm)
2001 6th Avenue South
Birmingham, AL 35233
(205) 328-9090
www.adanet.org

**American Society of Handicapped
Physicians (ASHP)**
Will Lambert, Director
3424 South Culpepper Court
Springfield, MO 65804
(417) 881-1570

American Veterans
(877) 726-8387
www.amvets.org

Association of Disabled Professionals
BCM ADP
London WC 1N3XX
www.adp.org

Association of Late-Deafened Adults
1145 Westgate Street, Suite 206
Oak Park, IL 60301
(877) 348-7537
www.alda.org

**Association on Higher Education and
Disability (AHEAD)**
University of Massachusetts, Boston
100 Morrissey Boulevard
Boston, MA 02125-3393
(617) 287-3880
www.ahead.org

Career Command Post
(877) 740-8380 - for transition active duty
personnel
www.careercommandpost.com
www.militaryheadhunter.com
www.trao.com
www.taonline.com

**Disabled Businesspersons Association
(DBA)**
www.disabledbusiness.com
info@disabledbusiness.com

**Dole Foundation for Employment of People
with Disabilities**
1819 H Street NW, Suite 340
Washington, DC 20006
(202) 457-0318

**Foundation for Science and Disability
(FSD)**
c/o Dr. E.C. Keller, Jr.
West Virginia University
Morgantown, WV 26506-6057

Gallaudet University
800 Florida Avenue, NE
Washington, DC 20002
(202) 651-5000
www.gallaudet.edu

**Helen Keller National Center for Deaf-
Blind Youths and Adults**
111 Middle Neck Road
Sands Point, NY 11050
(516) 944-8900
www.helenkeller.org

Job Accommodation Network (JAN)
P.O. Box 6080
Morganton, WV 26506
(800) 526-7234
http://janweb.icdi.wvu.edu

National Association of the Deaf
814 Thayer Avenue
Silver Spring, MD 20910
(301) 587-1788
www.nad.org

National Business and Disability Council
201 I.U. Willets Road
Albertson, NY 11507
(516) 465-1515
www.nbdc.com

National Center for Disability Services
www.ncds.org

National Easter Seals Society (NESS)
230 West Monroe Street, Suite 1800
Chicago, IL 60606
(312) 726-6200
(800) 221-6827
www.easter-seals.org

**National Institute for Rehabilitation
Engineering (NIRE)**
c/o Donald Selwin VP
P.O. Box 1088
Hewitt, NJ 07421
(800) 736-2216
(973) 853-6585
www.theoffice.net

**National Institute on Disability &
Rehabilitation Research**
400 Maryland Avenue SW
Washington, DC 20202
(202) 205-8134
www.ed.gov/offices/OSERS/NIDRR

National Organization on Disability (NOD)
910 Sixteenth Street NW, Suite 600
Washington DC 20006
(202) 293-5960
www.nod.org

National Technical Institute for the Deaf
Rochester Institute of Technology
52 Lomb Memorial Drive,
LBJ Building
Rochester, NY 14623
(585) 475-6400
www.rit.edu/NTID

**President's Committee on Employment of
People with Disabilities**
US Department of Labor
Office of Disability Employment Policy
Frances Perkins Building
200 Constitution Avenue NW
Washington, DC 20210
(202) 693-7880
www.dol.gov/odep

United Cerebral Palsy Association (UCPA)
1660 L Street NW, Suite 700
Washington DC 20036
(202) 776-0406
(800) 872-5827
www.ucp.org

Local "Linkage" Agencies

Included in this section is a listing of the types of local agencies, social service agencies, or human service agencies found in many communities. This list includes those that generally have a nation-wide presence, such as Goodwill Industries. There will be other regional or local ones. Check phone books, the library, or conduct an Internet search to locate appropriate agencies that represent the interests of women and minorities in the local community and locate contact information for those listed in this directory.

The following are some suggestions for establishing relationships:

- Contact representatives of the organizations and invite them for a facility tour. Review with them the types of positions and the job requirements.
- Send periodic announcements of job openings to these organizations.
- If the organizations offer job training or placement assistance, encourage the company to become involved by volunteering employee time or donating resources.
- Participate in job fairs or other community events.
- Consider sending the agencies a letter similar to the one on the following page if only occasional entry level hires are made.

SAMPLE INTRODUCTORY LETTER TO
OUTREACH AGENCIES
(SOCIAL SERVICE/HUMAN SERVICE ORGANIZATIONS)

Date

Name of Agency
Address

Dear _____ :

[Company] is dedicated to complying with its obligations of Equal Employment
Opportunity and Affirmative Action in all employment practices. We have an
on-going commitment to hire and develop the best people, based on job-related
qualifications. Accordingly, all applicants will be treated fairly. Our recruiting
and hiring procedures are free of unlawful discrimination based on race, color,
sex, age, disability status, religion, national origin, marital status, sexual
orientation, ancestry, political belief or activity, or U. S. veteran status.

As part of our Affirmative Action Program, we are committed to working within
those communities where we do business and encourage organizations such as
yours to refer qualified members of minority groups, women, disabled
individuals and veterans to us to fill our staffing needs. A list of our open
positions, along with information about the company, can be found on our web
site at www.**companyname**.com.

We appreciate your support in referring candidates to our company. Please call
me should you have any questions. My number is _____.

Sincerely,

Local "Linkage" Agencies

General

Private Industry Councils (PICs)
Local Job Banks and Training Services
Job Corp

Women's Organizations:

1. Women's Resource Centers or Agencies or Forums (in some locations may be affiliated with local colleges or universities) Within individual state Employment or Economic Security Agencies, departments supporting the employment of women EX: www.onlinewbc.gov

2. Women's Employment Resources Corporation www.wedc.org/wedclinks.htm

3. Women's Employment Projects or Networks www.miusa.org/intldev/women/ projects.htm

4. State/County Commissions on the Status of Women www.state.hi.us/hscsw/links.html

5. Displaced Homemakers or Displaced Homemakers Step by Step http://www.charmeck.org/ departments/womens+commission/displaced+homemakers/home. asp

6. YWCA (Women in Transition) www.charityvillage.com

7. League of Women Voters www.lwv.org/

8. National Council of Negro Women www.ncnw.org

9. Centers for Continuing Education for Women (may be affiliated with colleges and universities)

10. Department of Labor's Women Bureau www.dol.gov/wb/

11. National Association of Women www.nawbo.org

12. Women Employed-Job Bank www.womenemployed.org/

13. Office of Women's Services

14. American Association of University Women www.aauw.org

Minority Organizations

1. Urban League (Minorities)
   www.nul.org

2. NAACP (Blacks)
   www.naacp.org

3. League of United Latin American Citizens (LULAC) – Hispanic
   www.lulac.org

4. Minority/Women Business Enterprise

5. Council on Career Development for Minorities

6. Black/Hispanic Chambers of Commerce
   www.2chambers.com

7. Coalition of 100 Black Women
   www.ncbw.org/

8. Black Male Coalition

9. Black United Front www.nbufront.org

10. Hispanic Economic Development organizations www.hispanicbusiness.com

11. Hispanic Community centers

12. Youth Development organizations
    www.innercityyouth.org

13. Asian Community Services organizations
    www.sph.emory.edu/ bufordhwycorr/
    acs.html

14. Job Training programs

Individuals with Disabilities

1. Disabled American Veterans
   www.dav.org/main.html

2. State Vocational Rehabilitation Offices

3. Association for Retarded Citizens (ARC)
   www.thearc.org

4. Job Training programs

5. Easter Seals
   www.easter-seals.org

6. Goodwill Industries
   www.goodwill.org

Veterans

1. US Veterans Affairs Department
   www.va.gov/

2. Disabled American Veterans
   www.dav.org

3. Veterans Outreach centers http://
   grunt.space.swri.edu/ vaadmcen.htm

4. American Legion www.legion.org

5. Veterans of Foreign Wars www.vfw.org

6. Veterans Employment & Training centers
   www.jobsetc.org/ veteran_services.asp

State Agencies (Employment)

Alabama Department of Industrial Relations
649 Monroe Street
Montgomery, AL 36131
(334) 242-8990
FAX (334) 242-3960
www.dir.state.al.us

Alaska Employment Security Division
PO Box 25509
Jeneau, AK 99802-5509
(907) 465-2712
FAX (907) 465-4537
www.labor.state.ak.us/esd/home.htm

Arkansas Department of Employment Security
#2 Capital Mall, PO Box 2981
Little Rock, AR 72203-2981
(501) 682-2121
FAX (501) 682-2273
www.state.ar.us/esd/

Arizona Department of Economic Security
PO Box 6123-010A
Phoenix, AZ 85005-6123
(602) 542-5678
FAX (602) 542-5339
www.de.state.az.us/tp/portal.asp

California Employment Development Dept.
PO Box 826880, MIC83
Sacramento, CA 94280-0001
(916) 654-8210
FAX (916) 657-5294
www.edd.ca.gov/

Colorado Dept. of Labor and Employment
1515 Arapahoe, 2 Pk. Central,
Ste. 400
Denver, CO 80202-2117
(303) 620-4701
FAX (303) 620-4714
www.coworkforce.com

Connecticut Employment Security Division
200 Folly Brook Blvd.
Wetherfsield, CT 06109-1114
(860) 566-4384
FAX (860) 566-1520

District of Columbia Dept. of Employment Services
500 C Street, NW, Room 600
Washington, DC 20001
(202) 724-7000
FAX (202) 724-7112

Delaware Department of Labor
820 North French, Carvel State Bldg., 6th Floor
Wilmington, DE 19801
(302) 577-3950
FAX (302) 577-3996 www.delaware.gov/
agencies/DeptLabor/ Employment_Services

Florida Dept. of Labor & Employment Security
20212 Capital Circle, SE, Hartman Bldg.,
Suite 303
Tallahassee, FL 32399-2152
(904) 922-7021
FAX (904) 488-8930
www.floridajobs.org

Georgia Dept. of Labor
148 International Blvd., NE,
Suite 600
Atlanta, GA 30303
(404) 656-3011
FAX (404) 656-2683
www.dol.state.ga.us

Hawaii Dept. of Labor & Industrial Relations
830 Punchbowl Street, Room 321
Honolulu, HI 96813
(808) 586-8865
FAX (808) 586-9099
http://dlir.state.hi.us/

Idaho Dept. of Employment
317 Main Street
Boise, ID 83735
(208) 334-6110
FAX (208) 334-6430
www.labor.state.id.us

Illinois Dept. of Employment Security
401 S. State St., Room 615
Chicago, IL 60605
(312) 793-5700
FAX (312) 793-9306
www.ides.state.il.us

Indiana Dept. of Workforce Development
10 N. Senate Ave., Room 331
Indianapolis, IN 46204
(317) 283-5661
FAX (317) 233-1670
www.in.gov/dwd

Interstate Conference of Employment Security Agencies, Inc.
444 North Capitol St., NW
Washington, DC 20001
(202) 628-5588

Iowa Dept. of Employment Services
1000 E. Grand Ave.
Des Moines, IA 50319
(515) 281-5365
FAX (515) 281-4698
www.iowaworkforce.org

Kansas Dept. of Human Resources
401 SW Topeka Blvd.
Topeka, KS
(785) 296-7474
FAX (785) 296-0179
www.hr.state.ks.us

Kentucky Dept. for Employment Services
275 East Main St., 2nd Floor W.
Frankfort, KY 40621
(502) 564-5331
FAX (502) 564-7452

Louisiana Dept. of Labor
PO Box 94060
Baton Rouge, LA 70804-9040
(504) 342-3011
FAX (504) 342-3778
www.ldol.state.la.us

Maine Bureau of Employment Security
PO Box 309
Augusta, ME 04332
(207) 287-3788
FAX (207) 287-5292
www.state.me.us/labor

Maryland Dept. of Economics & Employment
1100 N. Eutaw St., Room 600
Baltimore, MD 21201
(410) 767-2400
FAX (410) 767-2986

Massachusetts Dept. of Employment & Training
Charles F. Hurley Bldg., Gov't Center
Boston, MA 02114
(617) 626-6600
FAX (617) 727-0315
www.detma.org

Michigan Employment Agency
7310 Woodward Ave.
Detroit, MI 48202
(313) 876-5500
FAX (313) 876-5587
www.michigan.gov/bwuc

Minnesota Dept. of Economic Security
390 N. Robert Street
St. Paul, MN 55101
(612) 296-3711
FAX (612) 296-0994
www.mnwfc.org

Missouri Division of Employment Security
PO Box 59
Jefferson City, MO 65104
(573) 751-3976
FAX (573) 751-4945
www.works.state.mo.us

Mississippi Employment Security Commission
PO Box 1699
Jackson, MS 39215-1699
(601) 961-7400
FAX (601) 961-7405
www.mesc.state.ms.us

Montana Dept. of Labor & Industry
1327 Lockey Ave., State Capital
Helena, MT 59620
(406) 444-3555
FAX (406) 444-1394
http://dli.state.mt.us

North Carolina Employment Security Commission
PO Box 25903
Raleigh, NC 27611
(919) 733-7546
FAX (919) 733-1129
www.ncesc.com/splash.asp

North Dakota Job Service
PO Box 5507
Bismark, ND 58506-5508
(701) 328-5000
FAX (701) 328-4000
www.state.nd.us/jsnd

Nebraska Dept. of Labor
PO Box 94600
Lincoln, NE 68509-4600
(402) 471-3405
FAX (402) 471-2318

Nevada Employment Security Division
500 E. Thrid St.
Carson City, NV 89713
(702) 687-4635
FAX (702) 687-3903
http://detr.state.nv.us/es/es_index.htm

New Hampshire Dept. of Employment Security
32 South Main Street
Concord, NH 03301
(603) 228-4008
FAX (603) 228-4145
www.nhes.state.nh.us

New Jersey Dept. of Labor
PO Box 110 John Fitch Plaza
Trenton, NJ 08625-0110
(609) 292-2323
FAX (609) 633-9271
www.state.nj.us/labor

New Mexico Dept. of Labor
PO Box 1928
Albuquerque, NM 87103-1928
(505) 841-8409
FAX (505) 841-8491
http://www3.state.nm.us/dol/ dol_home.html

New York Dept. of Labor
State Office Bldg Campus, Bldg 12, State Campus
Albany, NY 12240
(518) 457-2270
FAX (518) 457-6908
www.labor.state.ny.us/

Ohio Bureau of Employment Services
145 South Front Street
Columbus, OH 43215
(614) 466-2400
FAX (614) 466-5025
www.state.oh.us/odjfs/index.stm

Oklahoma Employment Security Commission
Will Rogers Memorial Office Building
Oklahoma City, OK 73152
(405) 557-0200
FAX (405) 557-7256
www.oesc.state.ok.us

Oregon Employment Department
875 Union Street, NE
Salem, OR 97311
(503) 378-3208
FAX (503) 947-1472
www.emp.state.or.us

Pennsylvania Dept. of Labor & Industry
Seventh & Forster Streets
Harrisburg, PA 17120
(717) 787-5279
FAX (717) 787-5785
www.dli.state.pa.us/landi/site/default.asp

Puerto Rico Bureau of Employment Security
506 Munzo Rivera Avenue
Hato Rey, PR 00918
(787) 754-5394
FAX (787) 763-2227

Rhode Island Dept. of Employment & Training
101 Friendship Street
Providence, RI 02903
(401) 277-3600
FAX (401) 277-1473
www.dlt.state.ri.us

South Carolina Employment Security Commission
PO Box 995
Columbia, SC 29202
(803) 737-2617
FAX (803) 737-2642
www.sces.org

South Dakota Dept. of Labor
700 Governors Drive
Pierre, SD 59501
(605) 773-3101
FAX (605) 773-4211
www.state.sd.us/dol/dol.asp

Texas Workforce Commission
RM 656 TEC Building,
101 East 15 St.
Austin, TX 78778
(512) 463-2222
FAX (512) 463-2652
www.twc.state.tx.us

Utah Dept. of Workforce Services
140 East 300 South
Salt Lake City, UT 84111
(801) 536-7401
FAX (801) 531-3785
http://jobs.utah.gov/

Vermont Dept. of Employment & Training
PO Box 488
Montpelier, VT 05602
(802) 828-4301
FAX (802) 828-4022
www.det.state.vt.us

Virginia Employment Commission
PO Box 1358
Richmond, VA 23218-1358
(804) 786-3001
FAX (804) 225-3923
www.vec.state.va.us

Virgin Islands Dept. of Employment &
Training
PO Box 3159
St. Thomas, VI 0083
(340) 773-1440
FAX (340) 773-1515
www.usvi.org/labor

Washington Employment Security
Department
PO Box 9046 Mail Stop KG-11
Olympia, WA 98504-5311
(360) 902-9300
FAX (360) 902-9383
www.wa.gov/esd

West Virginia Bureau of Employment
Programs
112 California Avenue
Charleston, WV 25305-0012
(304) 558-2630
FAX (304) 558-2992
www.state.wv.us/bep

Wisconsin Dept. of Workforce Development
PO Box 7946
Madison, WI 53707
(608) 266-7552
FAX (608) 266-1784
www.dwd.state.wi.us/default.htm

Wyoming Employment Resources Division
PO Box 2760
Casper, WY 82602
(307) 235-3650
FAX (307) 235-3293
http://onestop.state.wy.us/appview/

wjn_home.asp

Publications for Minorities, Women, and Individuals with Disabilities

The following is a listing of publications targeted to specific audiences. This list is not intended to be representative of the types of publications to consider for recruitment advertising needs. It is not intended to be an inclusive list. There may be other publications. As with any source, they are subject to change and thus the information presented herein may change from time to time. This information is presented as a representative sample and not an endorsement.

Affirmative Action Register
St. Louis, MO
(800) 547-0655 or (314) 991-1335
Monthly – Recruitment publication directed at women, minorities and the disabled

A Magazine: Inside Asian America
Metro East Publications
New York, NY
(212) 925-2123
Fax (212) 925-2896

Black Collegian
New Orleans, LA
(504) 523-0154
Bimonthly – African American students-all disciplines

Black Enterprise
New York, NY
(212) 242-8000
Fax (212) 886-9615
Monthly – African American business professionals and managers

Black EOE Journal
Yorba Linda, CA
(800) 487-5099
Quarterly – Professional and college students

Career Focus
Kansas City, MO
(816) 960-1988
Monthly – Minority college students and graduates

Careers & the Disabled
Huntington, NY
(516) 421-9469
3 times – Disabled professionals and college students

Careers and the Disabled Magazine
Equal Opportunity Publications
Hauppauge, NY
(516) 273-0036

Direct Aim
Kansas City, MO
(816) 960-1988
4 times – Minority college students
Dollars & Sense
Chicago, IL
(773) 468-4800
6 times – African American business professionals

Ebony
Chicago, IL
(312) 322-9200
Monthly – Urban African American consumers with above average incomes

Emerge
Washington, DC
(202) 608-2000
10 times – College-educated middle-class
African Americans

Equal Opportunity
Huntington, NY
(516) 421-9469
3 times – Minority college students and recent
graduates-all disciplines

Essence
New York, NY
(212) 642-0600
Monthly – Contemporary African American
women

Hispanic
Austin, TX
(512) 476-5599
Monthly – Upscale Hispanic Americans
Hispanic Business
Santa Barbara, CA
(805) 682-5843
Fax (805) 687-4546
Monthly – College-educated Hispanic
American professionals

Hispanic Times Magazine
Winchester, CA
(909) 926-2119
5 times – Hispanic American and Native
American professionals and college students

Independent Living Provider
Huntington, NY
(516) 421-9478
7 times – Able and disabled consumers

Jet
Chicago, IL
(312) 322-9200
Weekly – General interest publication geared
to African Americans

Mainstream
San Diego, CA
(619) 234-3128
10 times – Able and disabled consumers

Minority Business Entrepreneur
Torrance, CA
(310) 540-9398
Bimonthly – Business magazine aimed at
African American and Hispanic Americans

Minority MBA
Chicago, IL
(312) 236-2622
Annual – Minority MBA students

*Minority Organizations: A
National Directory*
Garrett Park Press, P.O. Box 190B
Garrett Park, MD 20896
Lists 9,700 minority organizations in the USA

National Hispanic Reporter
Washington, DC
(202) 898-4153
Hispanic Americans

Saludos Hispanos
Palm Desert, CA
(760) 776-1206
Quarterly – Focuses on education and role
models who have achieved success

Transpacific
Malibu, CA
(310) 589-2600
6 times – Asian Americans

Vista Magazine
Coral Gables, FL
(305) 442-2462
Monthly – Hispanic Americans – inserted into
English-language newspapers

Working Woman
New York, NY
(212) 445-6100
Monthly – Women business professionals

Winds of Change Magazine
AISES Publishing
Topeka, KS
(303) 492-8658
Associated with the American Indian Science
and Engineering Society

APPENDIX C

DEPARTMENTAL ANALYSIS/JOB AREA ACCEPTANCE RANGE (JAAR) ANALYSIS

The JAAR is a very useful tool in evaluating the distribution of women and minorities throughout a company's workforce. Analysis of the distribution of women and minorities in the company's workforce is required by 41 CFR£60-2.17 (b) Identification of Problem Areas. The analysis is helpful in identifying either potential discrimination issues or areas in the workforce where affirmative action is required.

How to Calculate the JAAR

The JAAR analysis compares the company's workforce contained in the AAP to an individual segment of that workforce. The individual segment may be a department or any organizational unit. The idea is that the distribution of women and minorities in the individual segment should be similar to that of the entire workforce. In practice, the analysis is usually made of the entire workforce broken down into white collar and blue-collar positions versus an individual department or organizational unit. The individual segment may be comprised of any grouping of employees; e.g., same job title, same job group, etc. The JAAR tests for situations in which the individual segment under analysis differs by more than ±20 percent from the workplace as a whole. If the analysis indicates that representation in the individual segment is within 20 percent of the representation of the entire workforce, the OFCCP will usually ignore that difference. If the JAAR analysis indicates that the representation of minorities or women in the individual segment is greater than 20 percent higher than that of the overall workforce, a "concentration" of women or minorities is said to exist in the individual unit. If representation of women and minorities in the individual segment is 20 percent lower than that of the overall workforce, an "under-representation" of women or minorities is said to exist in the individual segment.

The formula used in calculating the JAAR is:

$$JAAR = \frac{\text{Total Women or Minorities}}{\text{Total Employees}} \text{ x } \pm 20\%$$

$$EXAMPLE: \text{ JAAR} = \frac{15 \text{ Women or Minorities}}{100 \text{ Employees}} \text{ x } \pm 20\%$$

$$JAAR = (15\% \text{ x} \pm 20\%) = 12\% \text{ to } 18\%$$

The calculation of the individual segment in this example would be:

Women or Minorities in segment
Total employees in segment

EXAMPLE: $\frac{10 \text{ Women}}{40 \text{ employees in segment}} = 25\%$

Does the result of the segment analysis fall within the JAAR above? If yes, there is no apparent problem. If it is higher, there is a concentration of women in the segment; if lower, women are under-represented. In this example, the JAAR is 12 to 18 percent with 25 percent of the employees in the segment being women. There is, therefore, an apparent concentration of women in the segment.

Application of the JAAR

The JAAR, by itself, is not an indication of discrimination, nor is it an indication of a failure to take affirmative action. A JAAR analysis gives a good picture of how women and minorities are dispersed throughout the workforce. It identifies areas of concentration or under-representation of women and minorities and suggests areas where affirmative action may be appropriate. For example, if the JAAR indicates an under-representation of women in a certain department where availability figures indicate a high percentage of women are available for jobs in that department, two questions immediately come to mind. First, are the goals for those jobs groups appropriate? Second, what good faith efforts have been expended to overcome under-utilization of women in those job groups? If the JAAR indicates a high concentration of women in middle management jobs and an under-representation in top management jobs, is there a "glass ceiling" issue?

If and when problems are found as a result of a JAAR analysis, affirmative action must be taken to correct them. For example, if there is a concentration of women in one department, attempts to provide opportunities for them to be promoted or to transfer out of that department should be made. Likewise, if there is an under-representation of women or minorities in an area, appropriate action needs to be taken to remedy the situation. Keep in mind that under-representation of women or minorities indicated by a JAAR analysis does not require the company to set goals. The JAAR itself is not an absolute indicator that a problem exists.

It is a good idea to perform a JAAR analysis annually, using the same data period as the AAP update. Each area of concentration or under-representation identified by the analysis should be reviewed and a written explanation prepared and filed in the affirmative action file.

APPENDIX D

IMPACT RATIO ANALYSIS

Impact Ratio Analysis compares the rate of selection for different groups and determines the group which experiences the most advantageous rate.

For *positive employment decisions*, such as hires and promotions, the group experiencing the **higher** selection rate is the favored group.

For *negative employment decisions*, such as terminations/layoffs and demotions, the group experiencing the **lower** selection rate is the favored group.

For purposes of the company's Affirmative Action Program, Impact Ratio Analysis is performed to determine if adverse impact exists for Minorities and Females in the rate of selection for employment practices or opportunities.

OFCCP will focus on situations in which the selection rate for minorities or females is **less favorable** than the rate for others. OFCCP will conduct the IRA only when the rate for minorities or females is less favorable than for non minorities/males. In other words, for those employment decisions that are positive, the IRA will be conducted only if the selection rate for minorities or females is lower than the selection rate for non-minorities or males. For those employment decisions that are negative, IRA will be conducted only if the selection rate for minorities or females is higher than the selection rate for non-minorities or males.

Impact Ratio Analysis:

- determines the rate of selection for minorities and the rate of selection for non-minorities
- compares the minority selection rate to the non-minority selection rate
- determines the rate of selection for females and the rate of selection for males
- compares the female selection rate to the male selection rate
- determines if potential discrimination exists in some employment practice that adversely affects minorities and females.

Impact Ratio Analysis for positive employment practices identifies if minorities or females are selected less often than non-minorities or males.

Impact Ratio Analysis for negative employment practices identifies if minorities or females are selected more often than non-minorities or males.

- *The 80% Rule*, commonly referred to as the *4/5ths Rule*, should be used to determine if adverse impact exists.

- *Standard Deviation* analysis should be used to determine if identified adverse impact is statistically significant.

  Standard deviation is a statistical methodology. It helps to determine whether disparities in a series of employment decisions are likely to be occurring due to random chance or due to some other factor, such as deliberate discrimination. Each standard deviation represents a level of confidence that what is occurring is not due to chance.

  Standard Deviation analysis results should not be relied upon if the total population in the job group is less than 30 and the number of expected selections for the disadvantaged group is less than five (5).

- *Fisher's Exact Test* may also be used to determine if identified adverse impact is statistically significant. This Test can be used on all populations for all selection decisions. It is a more exact test than the Standard Deviation analysis but less commonly used by the OFCCP.

Employment Practices

Impact Ratio Analysis is performed for employment practices including:

Positive Employment Practices:

- Applicant flow
- Offers extended
- Hiring
- Competitive Promotions/Reclassifications or All Promotions
- Training

Negative Employment Practices:

- Voluntary terminations (not employer decision)
- Involuntary terminations
- Layoffs
- Total terminations

Impact Ratio Analysis is performed for each job group in the Affirmative Action Plan but it may also be performed by job title.

Personnel Transaction Data Required

- The IRA should be performed on the personnel transactions that occurred during the 12 months just prior to the beginning date of the current AAP.

- In an OFCCP compliance evaluation situation, the IRA should be performed on the personnel transaction that occurred from the first date of the AAP year to the date the compliance evaluation began (i.e. the date a scheduling letter from the OFCCP is received) if the company is six months or more into the current plan year.

- Personnel Transactions: For each job group, list number of:
  - Applicants
  - Offers extended
  - Hires
  - Competitive promotions or all promotions (see below)
  - Reclassifications
  - Terminations (total, voluntary, involuntary, and layoff each done separately)

OFCCP Performs IRA on:

- Selection procedures for:
  - Hires (against applicants)
  - Competitive promotions (against those who expressed interest in the promotion opportunity) or all promotions (against incumbent workforce)
  - Terminations (against incumbents)

Note: Depending on the size and nature of the workforce and the types of activity experienced, the scope of this analysis may be expanded.

- Each job group
- A comparison of males to females
- A comparison of total minorities to non minorities

Required Format For Personnel Transactions Data:

The transaction data should be listed for each selection decision by:

- Males
- Females
- Total Minorities
- Total Non Minorities
- Race (Minority Subgroup)

The Impact Ratio Analysis Formula (80% Rule)

Positive Decisions:

$$\frac{\text{Selection } \textbf{Rate} \text{ for minorities or females}}{\text{Selection } \textbf{Rate} \text{ for non} - \text{minorities or males}} =$$

If less than 80 %, there is Adverse Impact

Negative Decisions:

$$\frac{\text{Selection } \textbf{Rate} \text{ for minorities or females}}{\text{Selection } \textbf{Rate} \text{ for non} - \text{minorities or males}} =$$

If greater than 120%, there is Adverse Impact

Steps To Calculating The IRA Formula (80% Rule)

For each **personnel transaction** to evaluate, e.g.

- Hires (against applicants)
- Competitive promotions (against those who expressed interest in the promotion opportunity) or all promotions (against incumbent workforce)
- Terminations (against incumbents)

STEP 1:   Determine the selection rate:

The selection rate is the ratio of individuals from a specific group who are selected compared to all individuals in the pool

Selection Rate Calculation:

For Females:

$$\frac{\text{Specific Personnel Transaction}}{\text{Appropriate Pool}}$$
$$\text{(e.g. all females selected for hire)}$$
$$\text{(e.g. all applicants)}$$

For Males:

$$\frac{\text{Specific Personnel Transaction}}{\text{Appropriate Pool}}$$
$$\text{(e.g. all males selected for hire)}$$
$$\text{(e.g. all applicants)}$$

STEP 2:   Determine whether to continue with IRA formula:

Positive Decisions: If the minority or female rate is less than the non-minority or male rate, then perform IRA.

Negative Decisions: If the minority or female rate is greater than the non-minority or male rate, then perform IRA.

STEP 3: **Assuming the need to continue, calculate the IRA using the following formula:**

Positive Decisions: $\dfrac{\text{minority or female rate}}{\text{non - minority or male rate}}$

Negative Decisions: $\dfrac{\text{minority or female rate}}{\text{non - minority or male rate}}$

STEP 4: **Determine if Adverse Impact exists.**

If the result of Step 3 above is less than 80% for positive decisions, then adverse impact exists for the transaction for either minorities or females or both. If the result of Step 3 above is greater than 120% for negative decisions, then adverse impact exists for the transaction for either minorities or females or both.

OFCCP is concerned only when there is adverse impact for minorities or females, e.g., only when minorities and/or females are the un-favored group – the group that is not advantaged by the decision.

If adverse impact exists, it must be determined if it is statistically significant. A description of statistical significance follows the examples.

All employment decisions where adverse impact is noted should be investigated, regardless of whether or not statistical significance is indicated.

Examples (Note: These examples are provided for illustrative purposes only)

Example 1: IRA calculations for Hires compared to Applicants - Females

1. Determine the selection rate:

Selection Rate = Specific Personnel Transaction/
Number of Applicants in Job Group

Personnel transaction data:

Total Hires for Job Group 1A	=	35	→ Female	=	12
			→ Male	=	23
Total Applicants for Job Group 1A	=	300	→ Female	=	125
			→ Male	=	175

Calculate the rate:

Rate for Females   Female Hires /
Female Applicants

12 / 125 = 9.6%

Rate for Males   Male Hires /
Male Applicants

23 / 175 = 13.1%

2. Consideration to continue with IRA formula:

Positive Decisions: if the minority or female rate is less than the non-minority or male rate, then do the IRA

Negative Decisions: if the minority or female rate is greater than the non-minority or male rate, then do the IRA

Determination: Hiring rate for females is less than the hiring rate for males. Therefore, continue with the IRA formula.

3. IRA formula:

For Positive Decisions: Female rate / Male rate

Calculate the formula:

9.6% / 13.1% = 73.3% –   Adverse Impact exists for Females since the result is less than 80%.

Example 2: IRA for Hires compared to Applicants – Minorities

1. **Determine the selection rate:**

    Selection Rate = Specific Personnel Transaction /
    Number of Applicants in the Job Group

    Personnel transaction data:

    Total Offers Extended
    (Hires + Employment Declinations)
    for Job Group 1A   =   35 →   Minority   =   10
                            →   Non-Minority =   25

    Total Applicants for
    Job Group 1A   =   300 →   Minority   =   90
                            →   Non-Minority =   210

    Calculate the rate:

    Rate for Minorities   Minority hires /
                                     Minority applicants

                                     $10 / 90 = 11.1\%$

    Rate for Non-Minorities   Non-Minority hires /
                                     Non-Minority applicants

                                     $25 / 210 = 11.9\%$

2. Consideration to continue with IRA formula:

Positive Decisions: if the minority or female rate is less than the non minority or male rate, then do the IRA

Negative Decisions: if the minority or female rate is greater than the non-minority or male rate, then do the IRA

Determination: Hiring rate for minorities is less than the hiring rate for non-minorities. Therefore, continue with the IRA formula.

3. IRA formula:

For Positive Decisions: Minority rate / Non-Minority rate

Calculate the formula:

11.1% / 11.9% = 93.3% –   No Adverse Impact exists for Minorities since the result is greater than 80%.

Example 3: IRA calculation for Competitive Promotions against those who expressed interest in the promotion opportunity - Females

Note: *This is the preferred method of conducting the IRA for promotions if data has been maintained on those employees who have indicated an interest in a promotional opportunity. If this data is not available, then the IRA should be calculated using the method described in Examples 5 and 6 below.*

    1. Determine the selection rate:

        Selection Rate = Specific Personnel Transaction /
                    Pool of Employees in the Job Group who
                    Expressed Interest in all Promotional
                    Opportunities in the Job Group

        Personnel transaction data:

Competitive Promotions for
    Job Group 2A   =   30 → Female   =   4
                                  → Male   =   25

Total Employees who
    Expressed Interest
    in the Promotions   =   177 → Female   =   35
                                  → Male   =   142

Calculate the rate:

Rate for Females

Female promotions /
Females who expressed interest

$4 / 35 = 11.4\%$

Rate for Males

Male promotions /
Male who expressed interest

$25 / 142 = 17.6\%$

2. Consideration to continue with IRA formula:

Positive Decisions: if the minority or female rate is less than the non-minority or male rate, then do the IRA

Negative Decisions: if the minority or female rate is greater than the non-minority or male rate, then do the IRA

Determination: Promotion rate for females is less than the promotion rate for males. Therefore, continue with the IRA formula.

3. IRA formula:

For Positive Decisions: Female rate / Male rate

Calculate the formula:

$11.4\% / 17.6\% = 64.8\%$ − Adverse Impact exists for Females since the result is less than 80%.

Example 4:   IRA calculation for Competitive Promotions against those who expressed interest in the promotion opportunity - Minorities

Note: This is the preferred method of conducting the IRA for promotions if data has been maintained on those employees who have indicated an interest in a promotional opportunity. If this data is not available, then the IRA should be calculated using the method described in Examples 5 and 6 below.

1. **Determine the selection rate:**

    Selection Rate $=$ Specific Personnel Transaction /
    Pool of Employees in the Job Group who
    Expressed Interest in all Promotional
    Opportunities in the Job Group

    Personnel transaction data:

Competitive Promotions for
    Job Group 2A $=$ 30 ➔ Minority $=$ 6
                                     ➔ Non-Minority $=$ 25

Total Employees who
    Expressed Interest
    in the Promotions $=$ 177 ➔ Minority $=$ 35
                                   ➔ Non-Minority $=$ 142

Calculate the rate:

Rate for Minorities   Minority promotions /
Minorities who expressed interest

$6 / 35 = 17.1\%$

Rate for Non-Mihorities   Non-Minority promotions /
Non-Minorities who expressed
interest

$25 / 142 = 17.6\%$

2. Consideration to continue with IRA formula:

Positive Decisions: if the minority or female rate is less than the non-minority or male rate, then do the IRA

Negative Decisions: if the minority or female rate is greater than the non-minority or male rate, then do the IRA

Determination: Promotion rate for minorities is less than the promotion rate for non-minorities. Therefore, continue with the IRA formula.

3. IRA formula:

For Positive Decisions: Minority rate / Non-Minority rate

Calculate the formula:

$17.1\% / 17.6\% = 97.2\%$ — No Adverse Impact exists for Minorities since the result is less than 80%.

Example 5: IRA calculation for Promotions compared to the Incumbents in the job group - Females

Note: *This method should only be used if data has not been maintained on all employees who have expressed interest in the promotional opportunities.*

1. **Determine the selection rate:**

   Selection Rate = Specific Personnel Transaction /
   Incumbents in the Job Group

   Personnel transaction data:

Total Promotions for
    Job Group 2A   =   30 → Female   =   5
                                       → Male   =   25

Total Incumbents for
    Job Group 2A   =   177 → Female   =   36
                                       → Male   =   144

   Calculate the rate:

   Rate for Females   Female promotions /
                                        Females incumbents

                                        $5 / 36 = 13.9\%$

   Rate for Males   Male promotions /
                                        Male incumbents

                                        $25 / 144 = 17.4\%$

2. Consideration to continue with IRA formula:

Positive Decisions: if the minority or female rate is less than the non-minority or male rate, then do the IRA

Negative Decisions: if the minority or female rate is greater than the non-minority or male rate, then do the IRA

Determination: Promotion rate for females is less than the promotion rate for males. Therefore, continue with the IRA formula.

3. IRA formula:

For Positive Decisions: Female rate / Male rate

Calculate the formula:

13.9% / 17.4% = 79.9% — No Adverse Impact exists for Females since the result, rounded up to 80% is equal to 80%.

Example 6:   IRA calculation for Promotions compared to the Incumbents in the job group - Minorities

Note: *This method should only be used if data has not been maintained on all employees who have expressed interest in the promotional opportunities.*

1.   **Determine the selection rate:**
      Selection Rate =   Specific Personnel Transaction /Incumbents in the Job Group

      Personnel transaction data:

Total Promotions for
      Job Group 2A   =   30   ➔   Minority   =   4
                                   ➔   Non-Minority   =   25

Total Incumbents for
      Job Group 2A   =   177 ➔   Minority   =   35
                                   ➔   Non-Minority   =   142

      Calculate the rate:

      Rate for Minorities   Minority promotions /
                                    Minorities incumbents

                                    4 / 35 = 11.4%

      Rate for Non-Mihorities   Non-Minority promotions /
                                    Non-Minorities incumbents

                                    25 / 142 = 17.6%

160

2. Consideration to continue with IRA formula:

Positive Decisions: if the minority or female rate is less than the non-minority or male rate, then do the IRA

Negative Decisions: if the minority or female rate is greater than the non-minority or male rate, then do the IRA

Determination: Promotion rate for minorities is less than the promotion rate for non-minorities. Therefore, continue with the IRA formula.

3. IRA formula:

For Positive Decisions: Minority rate / Non-Minority rate

Calculate the formula:

11.4% / 17.6% = 64.8% – Adverse Impact exists for Minorities since the result is less than 80%.

Example 7: IRA for Total Terminations compared to Total Incumbents – Females

1. **Determine the selection rate:**

   Selection Rate =   Specific Personnel Transaction /
   Total Incumbents in the Job Group

   Personnel transaction data:

Total Terminations for
   Job Group 2A   =   20   ➜   Female   =   5
                             ➜   Male   =   15

Total Incumbents for
   Job Group 2A   =   177   ➜   Female   =   80
                             ➜   Male   =   97

   Calculate the rate:

   Rate for Females   Female terminations /
                               Female incumbents

                               5 / 80 = 6.3%

   Rate for Males   Male terminations /
                               Male incumbents

                               15 / 97 = 15.5%

2. Consideration to continue with IRA formula:

Positive Decisions: if the minority or female rate is less than the non-minority or male rate, then do the IRA

Negative Decisions: if the minority or female rate is greater than the non-minority or male rate, then do the IRA

Determination: The female rate is less than the male rate which means that males are terminating at a higher rate than females. Therefore, no adverse impact exists for females.

Example 8:   IRA for Total Terminations compared to Total Incumbents – Minorities

1.   **Determine the selection rate:**

> **Selection Rate =**   Specific Personnel Transaction /
> Incumbents in the Job Group

Personnel transaction data:

Total Terminations for
    Job Group 2A   =   20 ➔ Minority   = 9
                                  ➔ Non-Minority = 11

Total Incumbents for
    Job Group 2A   =   177 ➔ Minority   = 35
                                  ➔ Non-Minority = 142

Calculate the rate:

> *Rate for Minorities*   Minority terminations /
> Minority incumbents
>
> 9 / 35 = 25.7%
>
> *Rate for Non-Minorities*   Non-Minority terminations /
> Non-Minority incumbents
>
> 11 / 142 = 7.7%

2. Consideration to continue with IRA formula:

Positive Decisions: if the minority or female rate is less than the non-minority or male rate, then do the IRA

Negative Decisions: if the minority or female rate is greater than the non-minority or male rate, then do the IRA

Determination: Termination rate for minorities is greater than the termination rate for non-minorities. Therefore, continue with the IRA formula.

3. IRA formula:

For Negative Decisions: Non-Minority rate / Minority rate

Calculate the formula:

25.7% / 7.7% =333.8% –   Adverse Impact exists for Minorities since the result of 334% is greater than 120%

For those areas where adverse impact exists, determine if it is statistically significant.

	Females	**Minorities**
Hires	Yes	No
Competitive Promotions	Yes	No
All Promotions	No	Yes
Terminations	No	Yes

Note: The OFCCP may be interested in any incident of selection disparities, not just statistically significant disparities. For all areas where adverse impact has been identified, investigate each of the employment actions in that category to assure that no discriminatory decisions were made. The statistical significance of the adverse impact should also be determined.

Testing For Statistical Significance

What does "statistical significance" mean? It is a determination of whether disparities in a series of employment decisions are likely to be occurring due to random chance or due to some other factor, such as deliberate discrimination.

How is statistical significance measured? Two common methodologies are standard deviation and Fisher's Exact.

- Each standard deviation represents a level of confidence that what is occurring is not due to chance.

- If two events are compared using Standard Deviation analysis, the comparison measures how many actual standard deviations exist between the two events.

- If the comparison results in less than minus 2 standard deviations (i.e. -2.00 standard deviations or less), then there is acceptable confidence that the two events both occurred by chance.

- If the comparison results in greater than or equal to minus 2 standard deviations (i.e. -2.00 standard deviations or greater), then it can be inferred that the two events did not occur by chance and that there is an employment practice that is facially neutral that is causing the adverse impact. Where statistically significant adverse impact exists, the adverse impact must be explained by examining the underlying employment decisions that have been made in each transaction in the job group. If this is possible, then the apparent adverse impact has been satisfactorily eliminated. If it is not possible to explain the adverse impact, then the selection practice that is the underlying cause of the adverse impact must change.

- The OFCCP commonly uses minus 2.00 standard deviations or greater (i.e. -2.01, -2.02, etc.) as a benchmark in its compliance evaluations. The formulas to calculate standard deviations and Fisher's Exact are mathematically complex and are outside the scope of this roadmap. However, commercial software is commonly available for this purpose.

APPENDIX E

COHORT ANALYSIS

The Cohort Analysis is the comparison of the treatment of similarly situated individuals or groups.

STEP 1 -   Select a recent payroll period that reflects the current pay practices in use at the company.

STEP 2 -   Arrange the workforce by job title including all positions which perform the same or substantially the same duties in each group, even though their titles may not be the same.

STEP 3 -   Within the job title grouping, group together all males and then group together all females, arranging each group in salary order, from low to high.

STEP 4 -   Prepare a second listing, in the same manner as Step 3, grouped by minority and non-minority.

STEP 5 (a) -   Calculate the average (mean) pay of each of the four groups within the job title grouping.

     • Calculate the average pay for males, for females, for minorities, and for non-minorities

STEP 5 (b) -   Calculate the median pay of the four groups within the job title grouping.

     • Calculate the median pay for males, for females, for minorities, and for non-minorities

     The median pay is the point below which 50% of the pay rates lie and the point above which 50% of the pay rates lie.

STEP 6 -   Compare the average pay of the group of males to that of the females in the same job title

Compare the average pay of the minorities to the non-minorities.

Compare the median pay of the group of males to that of the females in the same job title

Compare the median pay of the minorities to the non-minorities.

STEP 7 -   Isolate those groups where minorities' and females' average pay is less than that for non-minorities and males.

Isolate those groups where the minorities' and females' median pay is less than that for non-minorities and males.

STEP 8 -   Determine the reasons that any male each group is paid more than any female.

Determine the reasons that any non-minorities who are paid more than minorities.

STEP 9 -   If, after performing the analyses, pay disparities are discovered for which no apparent business-related reasons exist, discuss the situation with other members of management and decide upon an appropriate course of action. Pay disparities which cannot be justified by business reasons should be corrected immediately.

This analysis should be limited to positions at one location, since factors such as cost of living differences, labor market conditions, etc. may require higher pay at one location than at another for identical positions.

APPENDIX F

RESOURCE INFORMATION

DEPARTMENT OF LABOR WEB-SITE
www.dol.gov

COPY OF FEDERAL REGULATIONS
www.access.gpo.gov/nara/cfr

AMERICA'S JOB BANK
www.ajb.dni.us

INFORMATION ON/LISTING OF "OTHER PROTECTED VETERANS"
vets100.cudenver.edu

EQUAL EMPLOYMENT OPPORTUNITY COMMISSION
www.eeoc.gov

EEO-1 WEBSITE
www.eeoc.gov/eeo1survey/

EO SURVEY WEBSITE
www.eosurvey.dol.gov/survey

Index

About the Authors

Thomas H. Nail is the President and founder of THOMAS HOUSTON associates, inc., a human resource management consultancy, which he began in 1978. The firm, whose core business is in equal employment opportunity and affirmative action, serves a nationwide client base from its offices in metropolitan Washington, DC and Fort Lauderdale, Florida.

A graduate of the University of Buffalo, Mr. Nail has been in the human resource field for over thirty years. Since writing his first affirmative action plan in the early 1970's, Mr. Nail and his staff have completed over 7,000 plans for clients in a multitude of industries in both the private and public sectors. He has directed over 450 OFCCP compliance reviews throughout the United States.

A longtime member of the Society for Human Resource Management (SHRM), Mr. Nail served on SHRM's Workplace Diversity Committee from 1981 to 2000. He assisted in the development and publication of SHRM's *Equal Employment Opportunity Manual for Managers and Supervisors* and has authored numerous articles and white papers for SHRM publications. In addition, Mr. Nail is the author of *Succeeding with Affirmative Action: A Comprehensive Desk Resource for Managers.* As a member of the Office of Federal Contract Compliance Program's National Liaison Committee, he assisted in writing the *OFCCP Federal Contract Compliance Manual.* He is frequently interviewed and quoted in national human resources publications.

Cornelia Gamlem, SPHR is President and founder of the GEMS Group ltd, a Human Resources consulting firm. She has over 20 years in the Human Resource Profession and worked for a Fortune 500 IT firm where she was responsible for managing policies, programs, and initiatives supporting best human resources and employment practices. Ms. Gamlem served on national task forces focused on issues of equal employment opportunity, affirmative action and workplace diversity. Since starting her practice, she has consulted with a wide range of clients on these issues.

A graduate of Marymount University, where she received a Masters Degree in Human Resource Management, Ms. Gamlem is also certified as Senior Professional in Human Resources (SPHR).

An active volunteer with the Society for Human Resource Management (SHRM), Ms. Gamlem has served on its National Board of Directors, its Global Forum Board of Directors, and chaired its National Workplace Diversity Committee. She has authored articles and white papers for SHRM and industry publications. Ms. Gamlem has presented at SHRM conferences, the American Bar Association and other business groups, has been interviewed by *The New York Times, Financial Times, Newsday,* and *Fortune,* and has testified before the Equal Employment Opportunity Commission. She teaches at colleges and universities in the Washington DC Metropolitan area.

177

OTHER BOOKS BY THESE AUTHORS

Roadmap to Success: Briefing Managers about Affirmative Action Results - An HR Professionals Guide, by Thomas H. Nail and Cornelia Gamlem

The second in the Roadmap series effectively guides the HR Professional in how to design a straightforward, consistent approach to presenting affirmative action program results to management staff. It provides an overview of AAP compliance and an explanation of the plan's analyses. Easy-to-use sample charts and formats to present the data to management staff are included.

Succeeding with Affirmative Action: A Comprehensive Desk Resource for Managers by Thomas H. Nail

This resource manual provides easy to understand information and answers about the entire affirmative action compliance process. Each topic contains a detailed introduction, followed by "Key Points to Remember," and a "Checklist of Audit Points." The desk resource contains copies of the applicable laws and regulations as well as sample forms and letters used during the compliance process.

VISIT US ON THE WEB

THOMAS HOUSTON associates, inc.
www.thomashouston.com

GEMS Group ltd
www.gemsgroup-hr.com